CW00985488

OBEDIENCE

Obedience

by

David Montague

The Pentland Press Limited
Edinburgh · Cambridge · Durham · USA

© David Montague 1999

First published in 1999 by
The Pentland Press Ltd.
1 Hutton Close
South Church
Bishop Auckland
Durham

All rights reserved.
Unauthorised duplication
contravenes existing laws.

British Library Cataloguing in Publication Data.
A catalogue record for this book is available
from the British Library.

ISBN 1 85821 693 1

Typeset by George Wishart & Associates, Whitley Bay.
Printed and bound by Antony Rowe Ltd, Chippenham.

To my God – without Whom
the writing of this book
would have been impossible

Setting the Scene

'Things are not what they used to be.'

A phrase that we have heard time and time again from the older generation.

'I'm not going to let my children out of my sight.'

Another phrase but this time coming from the younger generation.

We are living in a world, and certainly in our own country of Great Britain, when people are voicing their worries and concerns about the situation and environment in which they are living.

Safety on the roads, safety in the home, safety on the way to school, safety in the market place, safety at night, safety during the hours of daylight, safety out walking in the woods, safety in the crowded streets. Wherever people are, of whatever age, they are concerned about their safety from all kinds of dangers.

What are these dangers that people are concerned about?

They vary according to where people are and what they are doing or want to do.

Old folk, and the not so old, are frightened to go out at night alone for fear of being mugged.

Houses, if people can afford it, are double locked, security bolts are fitted to all the windows, spy holes are fitted to the front door and still there is the fear of their houses being broken into. We read of intruders who have broken into a house and when caught red-handed attack the owner and savagely beat him and leave him unconscious.

Another situation involved a man who remonstrated with a

1

youth who was sitting on the bonnet of his new car. This man was beaten and left to die in the road.

In another reported case a couple posing as doctors forced their way into the home of an 82-year-old woman, beat her unconscious and stole her ear-rings and 74p.

A widow of eighty-eight who sought refuge in Britain after her parents died in Stalinist Russia and she herself was forced into slave labour in Nazi Germany was sexually assaulted in her own home. She was left in a critical condition, covered in blood, and had been badly beaten around the face.

Then there is the danger of rape, perhaps one of the vilest crimes outside of murder. Rape committed during the course of burglary, rape committed on the spur of the moment by an individual, rape committed by two or more men or youths who drag their victim away to an isolated venue and violate her body.

And murder. Crimes of passion. Wives killed by jealous husbands or ex-husbands. Husbands killed by new boy-friends. People killed for money. People killed because someone has lost his or her temper. Children killed for lust. People killed for what appear to be motiveless crimes.

So we could go on. The media, radio, television and newspapers, give us a daily account of one or other of these crimes and we listen to them but then they pass over us unless we are personally involved. We may make some comment about the state of society today, hope the culprits are caught but then get on with watching our favourite programme on television.

So what are we going to do about this? Each political party claims to be the party of Law and Order but the situation doesn't seem to be getting any better. When a criminal is apprehended and brought to justice the punishment in many cases doesn't fit the crime, or so the victims believe. Prisons are overcrowded and in need of modernisation. Dangerous criminals escape and the public are warned not to approach them, even if they could recognize them! Others appear to be released well before they have served their deserved sentence.

Then Dunblane came and the tragedy of those young children and their teacher being killed by a maniac following on from the other madman who killed the people in Hungerford several years earlier.

Philip Lawrence, Headmaster of a London school, was killed outside his own school trying to ensure safety for his pupils. Now his wife, Frances, calls for a look into the whole morality within the country.

Parliament has now banned certain categories of handguns with others calling for a ban on all guns.

With the problems of discipline at The Ridings School in Halifax we now have a call for the re-introduction of the cane.

So, who or what is at fault?

Is it the Government?

Is it the Lawmakers?

Is it the programmes on Television?

Is it the wrong diet we are having?

Is it a lack of exercise?

Is it because we were born in the South or the North of the country?

Is it because of unemployment?

Is it the Teachers?

Is it the Parents?

Is it no one's fault and it's just the way things are going at the moment?

Everyone is agreed that something has to be done, but what?

When an election is coming the Political Parties jump on the 'Law and Order' bandwagon. Some of them would say they have never been off it.

There is an admonition to parents to bring up their children in a disciplined manner. This is a full time task for families where there are two parents. Where there is just one parent, and in most of these cases this is the mother, it becomes an almost impossible task, even though some do succeed.

Education in morality is now being advocated in all schools as an addition to the curriculum.

All of these suggested solutions have their good points but they will never solve the underlying problem.

Why not?

As has been said, it's not the guns nor the knives nor the fists which are the problem, it's people.

So when we are enjoined to go 'Back to Basics' or return to the old morality how far back should we go and what should we use as our guide?

I believe we have to return to the very beginning of time to find our answer. We need to go back to when God created the world and placed man on it. We need to return to the Bible where we can find some of the answers to the problems we face in the latter end of the twentieth century.

In the book of Genesis, in the early chapters, we find there an account of creation. This is not a scientific account – the Bible was never intended to be that – but it shows how God created the world and then man.

Adam and Eve, the first human beings on our planet earth, were set in the Garden of Eden, a Paradise. They were free to do whatever they liked except for one thing. They were forbidden to eat from the tree of knowledge of good and evil, for on the day that they ate from it they would die.

Eve was tempted by Satan, the Devil.

She listened to him. He sounded very plausible. 'You won't die,' he said, 'God wouldn't really mean that.'

The tree looked good for food, it was a delight to the eyes, it was to be desired to make one wise. So Eve picked some of its fruit, gave some to her husband, Adam, and they both ate. Immediately their eyes were opened to the good and evil in the world just as God had said.

They had been disobedient and it was this first ever act of disobedience that caused all the problems for them. Adam blamed Eve, Eve blamed the Devil, but the deed was done.

Punishment followed this act of disobedience. Adam and Eve were no longer permitted to remain in Paradise. They were punished for what they had done.

In all the talk we hear today about the problems we face in our country these are the two things we have to face up to, obedience and punishment.

It's because of disobedience that all these problems are here today.

Disobedience to parents.

Disobedience to school teachers.

Disobedience to the Laws of the Land.

Disobedience to the Laws of God.

All of these are in reality enshrined in that last one, disobedience to the Laws of God, because God has stated that we should obey the Law of the Land, that we should obey those in authority over us and that we should obey our parents.

The problem is we don't like being told what to do. We don't all acquiesce like Richard Bucket to the requests of Hyacinth in *Keeping Up Appearances*. For whatever reason, most of us want to do our own thing and not be told what we should be doing by other people.

In fact, to return to the Garden of Eden, there were no problems there until disobedience entered into the lives of Adam and Eve.

We don't know how long they lived in that Paradise until they gave in to temptation. During that time, however, they experienced no sickness or illness, they suffered no pain, they had no financial problems, they had no housing difficulties, they did not suffer from the extremities of temperature, they could go out without having to secure their property and when they went out they were in no danger of being mugged. They were, in fact, in Paradise.

Then temptation came and they gave in to it. Why?

Did Adam and Eve have any psychological problems?

It certainly couldn't have been their upbringing!

It wasn't their social environment.

They weren't short of money.

They weren't unemployed.

The answer is that it was plain, straightforward disobedience, what the Bible calls *sin*.

What happened?

Their eyes were opened to good and evil.

They were sent out from Paradise.

They hid from God.

They were punished.

God had created a perfect environment in which His created beings could have lived for ever without disease or death. Now that had all changed and because of their transgression disease and death would be in the world until the end of time.

The Bible relates the story about how God set about restoring man to a right relationship with Him that was broken by man's sin in the Garden of Eden.

What has that got to say to us today as we approach the end of the second millennium?

The following chapters set out the answers I believe are found in the pages of Scripture as to how we should be living out our lives and what should happen if we transgress God's laws.

Purposes of the Law

In a Democracy the Government of the day makes laws, amends laws and changes laws according to the will of Parliament who are elected by the people. There is never unanimous agreement as to whether these laws are good or right and so they are constantly changing or being revised.

Disobedience to these laws can lead to punishment if the offender is apprehended. Sentence is then proclaimed by the magistrate or judge according to the severity of the offence or crime.

This can lead to an appeal, either because the sentence is deemed too severe or in some cases too lenient.

The purpose of the sentence can be threefold, namely the protection of the public, the punishment of the criminal and hopefully, his reform. That there are so many criminals who, on their release from prison, re-offend, shows that the system is not working as it should. In an ideal world there would be no prisons, because there would be no people who had offended against the law.

Even in a primitive society there would soon have to come into being a code of ethics if the people were going to live in some sort of harmony with each other.

Because we live in a democracy we have a great deal of freedom, but that freedom does not extend to breaking the law because we could well be hurting other people and if we do that we lay ourselves open to being punished.

Where the law works then it is obviously good. In England we drive on the left hand side of the road and there are certain rules set out in the Highway Code which we have to abide by if we want to avoid having an accident. On a dual carriageway we have to drive on the left along with all the other traffic going in the same direction. If we enter the dual carriageway in the opposite direction it wouldn't be very long before we met vehicles coming towards us and we would be in difficulties, if not killed.

The Ten Commandments were given by God to Moses on Mount Sinai to take down to the Israelites to show them how they were to live. The first four revealed the duty the people had towards God and the last six the proper relations with man.

When Jesus came he didn't do away with the Law; he said he came to fulfil it, to make it complete. This is the Law by which we should be living in our country today if we claim to be a Christian country.

It can be seen quite clearly that all of these commandments are broken by some of the people and some of these commandments are broken by all of the people. None of us is perfect, all of us have fallen short of what the Law requires so we are all guilty and so are in need of punishment.

Is this so even if we were to break only one of the commandments? The answer to this is yes. An illustration may help to make this clear. If a chandelier is hanging by a chain made up of ten links and one of them broke, then the chandelier would fall to the ground. In a similar manner, if we break just one of the commandments then we have broken the Law and are guilty.

So the Law shows us how we ought to live just as it was intended at the time God gave the Ten Commandments to Moses.

God it was who had brought the Israelites out of bondage in Egypt and it was to Him that they should have been turning, but when Moses came down from Mount Sinai he discovered that they had persuaded Aaron to let them build a golden calf with the idea of worshipping it.

People have been worshipping idols throughout all time whether they are made with human hands or whether they are other objects or money or position in life.

When Paul was in Athens he saw idols of every description on Mars Hill including one to an unknown god in case they had left one deity out. They were very superstitious, Paul told them, and then proceeded to tell them about Jesus and how he had died on the cross outside Jerusalem for all and that if they believed in him as Lord and Saviour then they would inherit eternal life.

The Law also showed that they were not to treat the name of God in a disrespectful manner.

Commandments from five through to ten are dealing with our relationships with our fellow human beings.

The Law shows us how we ought to live but we, just like the Israelites of old, have not obeyed the Law and are guilty.

How do these Commandments help us to see our way forward today?

Crime

What is a crime?

What is a sin?

What is the difference?

A crime is an act committed in direct opposition to the Law of the Land.

A sin is an act committed in direct opposition to the will of God.

Peter, in the Book of Acts, states that we are to obey God rather than man. This is not an open defiance to the Law of the Land but where the Law of the Land and the Law of God differ, then the Law of God is the one to be obeyed.

For example, Daniel prayed five times a day although a decree had been made by King Darius that this was forbidden. He had committed a crime but he had not sinned.

Where two consenting adults commit an act of homo-sexuality in private they have sinned before God but they have not committed a crime against the Law of the Land.

Many crimes are therefore sins but not every sin is a crime and not every crime is a sin.

We have all sinned and come short of the standard that God requires of us and are in need of forgiveness by Him. A later chapter takes up this theme and what we can do about it.

Both sins and crimes are punishable offences. God alone is able to punish sins but He has handed over the punishment of crimes to His human creations. The Bible gives some guidelines as to what should be done. The Old Testament talks about an 'eye for an eye and a tooth for a tooth'. What this means is that the punishment should fit the crime.

When Jesus uses this illustration in his Sermon on the Mount and told them that they weren't to retaliate he was talking to the disciples individually. He did not mean that there was to be no punishment if the Law of the Land was broken. He had already stated earlier in this Sermon that he hadn't come to abolish the Law and the Prophets but that he had come to fulfil them.

Indeed if he had meant that the Law was to be abandoned it wouldn't have been very long before the Roman authorities came to hear about it and his ministry would have ended as soon as it had begun.

It is crimes of violence and crimes against the person that I really want to concentrate on in the next few chapters.

Murder

When I was a boy I used to travel all over London with a friend. We bought a ticket for sixpence (6d or 2.5p today) which enabled us to use unlimited numbers of buses. We went to the bus depots and collected bus numbers. Another ticket for the same price allowed us to use buses south of the River Thames as well as north. An additional ticket allowed us to use the tube train system. We never felt afraid to travel on our own. In fact it never even entered our minds that there was a possibility of being attacked or assaulted let alone being murdered. But I never let my children travel on their own anywhere and when we take out the grandchildren they are not allowed out of our sight.

My wife will not walk anywhere off the beaten track on her own and she even doesn't like going out in the car at night when she is unaccompanied.

I guess this state of affairs is mirrored up and down the country in town and village. A walk in the woods, which used to be very pleasant, can now be a horrifying experience for anyone going on his or her own.

Tunnels under a main road which were placed there to prevent people being knocked down by vehicles have become places which people won't use for fear of being attacked, either by individuals or gangs of youths.

The Moors murders and the women killed by Fred and Rosemary West may have been the ones that hit and stayed in the headlines for a long time and, indeed, are still mentioned today, but others are no less horrific.

How many boys used to go fishing on their own, quite often in isolated places? In July 1995 two schoolboys were found murdered in woodland near their homes after they failed to return from a fishing trip. They had travelled about one and a half miles from their homes to go fishing.

Everyone around the area where they came from was

devastated because fishing was a pastime enjoyed by many boys in the area.

In June 1994 a man sexually assaulted and then murdered a three-year-old girl he saw playing near her home. He had seized her and dragged her to his flat before killing her.

In January 1996 a teenager was kicked to death on a street corner near his home when he confronted a youth and a young man who had insulted his father.

These are only three of the many incidents that happen regularly up and down our land. Sometimes the criminal or criminals are caught and if there is sufficient evidence against them they are convicted and sentenced to a certain number of years in prison or for life, which doesn't normally mean what it says.

Whatever else it does, it certainly doesn't deter others from equally bestial murders.

Then there are murders committed during the course of robbery where the victims are shot or stabbed or hit over the head.

Some rape victims are murdered; some punch-ups lead to people being killed; some burglars kill the inhabitants of the homes they intend to rob.

Why does it go on?

I haven't even mentioned the murders that occur when someone loses his or her temper and lashes out with whatever weapon happens to be nearest.

Indeed, the whole of the human scene can be seen to be characterized by a lawlessness and a lack of respect for authority.

What does the Bible have to say about this?

The Apostle Paul wrote these words to the Believers in Rome:

> Let every person be subject to the governing authorities. For there is no authority except from God, and those that exist have been instituted by God. Therefore he who resists the authorities resists what God has appointed, and those who resist will incur judgement. For rulers are not a terror to good conduct, but to bad. Would you have no fear of him who is in authority? Then do what is good and you will receive his approval, for he is God's servant for your good. But if you do wrong, be afraid, for he does not bear the sword in vain; he is the servant of God to execute his wrath on the wrongdoer. (Romans 13 v 1-4 RSV).

These verses make it absolutely clear that when individuals commit acts which are not lawful then they are responsible to God for their wrongdoing. God has ordained human governments as His divinely appointed agents to ensure that justice is done in the land, that the laws are obeyed and where they are not then suitable punishments are meted out to those who have transgressed.

These punishments must be fair and fit the severity of the crime. Hence the injunction in the Old Testament was an 'eye for an eye and a tooth for a tooth', the just punishment for the crime.

Punishment can either be too heavy, too light or just right.

There may even be some Christians who say that punishment is inconsistent with love but that is not what is found in the Bible and we have to remember that God is a God of Judgement as well as a God of Love.

What then is the just punishment for the crime of murder?

Humanly speaking, to fine a murderer a sum of money,

however large, and then set him or her free for such a foul crime would be ludicrous.

To punish him or her more would be to involve some kind of torture which would be totally outside of human reason and is certainly not advocated by the Bible.

The just, fair and equitable punishment for taking a life is Capital Punishment and authority for this is there in the Bible. God laid down that principle very early on in the Book of Genesis when He was speaking to Noah: 'Whoever sheds the blood of man, by man shall his blood be shed; for God made man in His own image.' (Genesis 9 v 6 RSV).

That is not to say that every person who kills another human being should suffer the death penalty but it is there as a standard to show the sanctity of life. In fact, not everyone who took the life of an individual in Biblical times lost his or her life as a punishment. Other punishments took their place.

When Cain killed Abel, God told him he would become a fugitive and a wanderer on the earth. Cain told the Lord that his punishment was greater than he could bear.

After Moses had killed the Egyptian who was beating a Hebrew he hid his body in the sand. Moses must have been observed because Pharaoh heard about it and wanted to kill him but Moses fled from Pharaoh and stayed in the land of Midian.

Neither Cain nor Moses suffered the death penalty and certainly, in Moses' case, there were mitigating circumstances.

And there may well be mitigating circumstances for some murders that take place today and not everyone who kills someone else should suffer the death penalty. There may even be some cases where someone who takes a life is not guilty of a crime at all and should go free.

In another chapter there are some hypothetical cases of murders and what I consider the verdict should be.

Rape

The cases of rape that we read about in the newspaper and hear on the radio and see on the television appear, to my mind, to be increasing in number. As I have already indicated, some of them are followed by the murder of the person concerned.

In February 1996 a man with a 'mission' to rape and humiliate white middle-class women was given five life sentences for crimes committed after his release from a secure mental hospital.

In September 1996 five young men were jailed at the Old Bailey for periods ranging between thirty months and ten years for raping a girl seven times. At the end of this time, and possibly earlier, they will be released. The girl involved may be traumatized for life.

Were the penalties adequate?

Many people would think not. Leaving aside the relatives of rape victims who, understandably, want to see heavy sentences, the amount of imprisonment they received would appear not to fit the crime.

What, then, should they have received?

At the very least, castration, so that they would not be able or want to offend again in a similar manner. Or how about capital punishment in the worst case scenarios? They may not have killed the person physically but they have destroyed something very precious in a young woman or even traumatized an older woman. Which would be nearer to the equal punishment?

And how about those cases where a diet of pornography is involved?

If ever there is someone who will be high in the annals of heaven then surely it will be Mrs Mary Whitehouse. Often, so it seemed, she stood alone when she complained about the depravity that was, and still is, portrayed as art in the cinema, on the television and in the printed word.

Thomas Hamilton appeared to be steeped in pornography when he committed that terrible crime in Dunblane. Should not the purveyors of the material found in his possession have stood trial in his place and, if found guilty, undergone what punishment? Capital punishment perhaps? Is that going too far? Ask the parents of those children killed at Dunblane School.

Rape and pornography, certainly as we know them today, hardly ever appear in the Bible. There were laws in Exodus about what should happen if a virgin was seduced (Exodus 22 v 16-17 RSV) but no incidents of rape or gang rape as we read about it today are recorded in the pages of Scripture.

Pornography, with its appeal to the basest instincts in mankind, did not exist in Biblical times. There were no visual means like television as we have available today to titillate the senses. Undoubtedly it has the means to corrupt but to prove this in a court of law can be difficult.

Some of the films being produced and released are pornographic in the extreme, despite what some of the producers would have us believe. You do not have to see them

17

to appreciate that fact. We know that fire burns but we don't have to stick our hands in the flames to experience that. We know that water can drown but we don't have to try it for ourselves before advising people against attempting it. In a similar fashion we know that pornography corrupts so we don't have to view pornographic material to prove that fact.

However, it may be more difficult to prove in a court of law that some, if not many, of those who commit crimes of rape have been steeped in pornography and that this has played a large part in their committing the crime. If it could be proved, should not those purveyors of pornographic material be equally guilty alongside the actual perpetrator of the crime?

It is a fact that keeping and stroking animals that are kept as pets is very therapeutic. I imagine that it would be very difficult to prove this in a court of law but that does not invalidate the experience or make it less true.

As there are degrees of murder so there can also be degrees of rape.

In September 1996, five young men who raped a Japanese student were jailed for varying terms. They had put her through a quite inhuman experience which could well traumatize her for life. At the very least all of them should have been castrated and been handed life sentences, thus putting them out of reach of other women for the remainder of their natural lives, regardless of their age – another subject I take up in a later chapter. Or would capital punishment have been more humane? At least it would have achieved the same objective and have saved the country a great deal of money.

'What about the Christian view of forgiveness?' I hear a great number of people shouting at me. Yes, of course there can be forgiveness if there is repentance. But if there is no repentance there can be no forgiveness. That is Biblical. I will also take up this question in a later chapter.

At the opposite end of the spectrum there is rape which can occur even in a marriage. This is not only much more difficult to prove but even if proven must surely carry a completely different level of punishment.

In between these two extremes of rape there is an entire range that have to be heard and dealt with as and when they occur, always bearing in mind that the punishment must fit the crime.

Armed Robbery

For the first thirteen years of my working life I was employed by one of the large clearing banks, less my two years in National Service. Now there's a thought for help in learning obedience! How about bringing back National Service?

For most of my years in the Bank, Capital Punishment was in operation. I left the employment of the Bank in 1961 and Capital Punishment was finally abolished in 1969. For quite a number of my eleven years working in the Bank I was employed on the counter dealing with customers and, of course, cash.

There was never a thought in my mind that we would be robbed but when Capital Punishment was nearing its inevitable end and when it finally went, what happened? Armed robbery started to occur. Slowly but inexorably surely, security men and Banks and other financial institutions were targeted.

What, then, is the position today?

Not only is armed robbery commonplace but in many cases the robbers have no compunction whatsoever in shooting to kill anyone who stands in their way.

Banks have gone from having open counters where personal contact with customers is so much better, to first of all the return of metal grilles and then to bullet-proof glass.

Obviously there is no deterrent to such crimes being perpetrated and it certainly seems to be that they are correct in their assumption because few are apprehended and when they are caught and the case proven against them the punishment doesn't fit the crime.

What has gone wrong?

Again it is the lack of obedience to the law in the first place and when a successful case is brought against the criminals the punishment is not sufficient and doesn't deter further similar crimes being committed. In other words the punishment neither fits the crime nor acts as a deterrent.

Armed robbery can of course be against the individual as well as the employees of an institution.

It does not always mean that guns are used. It could be knives or other implements that have a lawful use in their right context.

The ancient art of pickpocketing (although I don't advocate its legality!) never carried the overtones of violence that encapsulate so much of today's theft. Mugging is the name of the game and the age or sex of the victim seems rarely to be taken into account.

The brutality handed out to the victim sometimes has to be read about to be believed. The banning of all weapons of violence is neither practical nor reasonable because in many cases it is the weapons attached to the ends of the human arms that have caused all the damage.

Burglary

There is nothing new about theft from houses. It certainly goes back to Biblical times. Jesus, when talking to his disciples about his second coming to earth, spoke about this which we find recorded in Matthew's gospel. ' "Know this," Jesus said, "that if the householder had known in what part of the night the thief was coming, he would have watched and would not have let his house be broken into." ' (Matthew 24 v 43 RSV).

When Judas came to the Garden of Gethsemane to betray Jesus, he was accompanied by a great crowd with swords and clubs. Jesus said to them, ' "Have you come out as against a robber, with swords and clubs to capture me?" ' (Matthew 26 v 55 RSV).

In these days of unemployment, burglary is a growth industry. You don't have to have a great deal of training, you just learn the trade as you go along!

Some burglars are neat and tidy and even leave a note thanking the householders for their pickings.

Others are less so and turn every drawer out to discover if anything valuable is placed there.

Then there are the vandal burglars who not only turn everything out but then destroy it or leave graffiti all over the place or even set light to the furniture and destroy it that way.

So what happens?

The insurance companies put up their premiums.

Double-glazing firms do a roaring trade.

Businesses providing various kinds of alarm systems are selling their wares.

All shapes and sizes of locks for doors, windows and anywhere else which is vulnerable are recommended to be fitted.

Various sorts of warning lights are attached to the outside of houses which are activated when people come near the region of the house.

Police advise householders to set up Neighbourhood Watch communities.

And still houses are broken into.

In some cases the burglaries occur when the owners are actually in residence. This can lead to violence and even injury or death may occur.

So what can be done about it apart from the remedies mentioned above?

First of all the law of liability has to be changed. At the moment if any burglar is injured or even killed by the householder then the householder is responsible for his actions and has to prove that he used only reasonable force. What nonsense! I say that the occupant of a house should be able to defend himself in any way he likes if he apprehends a burglar in the act of burglary. The 'burglar' should have to prove that he had a legitimate reason to be in someone else's house. Someone breaking and entering has forfeited any rights to protection from the law.

If a burglar knew that anything could be done to him if he entered a house illegally, I'm sure he would think twice before committing himself to such an act.

Other Crimes

There are, of course, many other crimes which involve violence in one way or another and it would be impossible to cover all of them in detail but the above crimes of murder, rape, armed robbery, mugging and burglary are the ones that concern most people and prevent them from enjoying life to the full, especially old folk who live on their own.

I make no mention of other criminal activities which do not involve violence such as tax evasion, theft from employers, embezzlement and other 'book' crimes.

Then there are 'crimes' which are not considered crimes in the eyes of many people at all, such us unfaithfulness in marriage and practising homosexuality but they are certainly sins in the eyes of God.

The break-up of a marriage where there are children involved can ruin the lives of those children and because of the instability involved can often lead to crime.

Statistics can be said to prove whatever you want them to but my guess is that the number of children who turn to crime from a stable, loving, two-parent family are far fewer than those from broken homes. Of course there are always going to be exceptions but the family unit is the most important and every effort should be made by the State as well as by the parents to keep them together. Tax incentives should always be in favour of a married couple and not single parents where that singleness is a deliberate choice. Widows and the fatherless should be a concern not only of the near relatives but should be helped all they can by the State. There is certainly Biblical authority for that because seven men were selected to carry out just that duty

23

so that the disciples could carry on with their task of proclaiming the gospel. The proclamation of the Good News went hand in hand with helping those in need.

We live in a society which has wandered far away from the commandments given by God to Moses for the people of Israel all those years ago and which have never been rescinded and which are as much applicable to us today as they were for the Israelites in the time of Moses.

Back to Basics

I have already indicated that punishment can be more severe than the crime committed, less than the crime committed or equal to the crime committed and it is the purpose of the Law that justice is carried out. Otherwise, as has so often been quoted, the Law is an ass.

We have travelled far, and rightly so, from hanging a person for stealing a sheep. But sheep-stealing is still a crime. What is the punishment that should be meted out to someone caught in this very act?

We often read that the courts do not have the jurisdiction to impose a certain punishment on an individual because their hands are tied for some reason or other. Why?

If justice is not being carried out in these cases then, once again, the Law has to be altered.

Criminal acts are being carried out today by youngsters below the age of responsibility so the courts are again limited in what punishment they can give. Yet some of these criminal acts are heinous in the extreme.

Then we read about the maximum sentence that can be

OBEDIENCE

given for a certain crime and some judges, believing this to be
unjust, have to state that their hands are tied and they are
unable to impose the sentence justified by the case.

So what can or should be done?

I believe that maximum and minimum sentences should be
scrapped entirely and judges be free to impose whatever
sentence they consider is justified by the case they are judging.
Whilst realising that this gives the judge enormous powers,
surely it is preferable to their being handicapped by the
restrictions of the law. Maybe the sentence should be imposed
by three judges who come to a united decision so that once
again no one individual has to bear the entire burden of
sentencing.

Under this free system of punishment, in theory it would
mean that capital punishment, which in my opinion must
return if we are ever to have a safe society in which to live,
could be imposed on someone who steals from a shop. But that
would not be justice. On the other hand neither is it justice if
someone who kills a cashier in an armed raid on a Building
Society is fined £10.

What then is the answer?

First of all, what are the number of different punishments
that at the moment can be imposed? Very broadly they are just
two. The first is deprivation of liberty or imprisonment and the
second is a fine. There are others, but they are based more or
less on these two.

I would suggest putting punishment into three categories.

The first would be capital punishment. This does not have to
be hanging. There are many other methods that can be used
but the principle of a man losing his life for taking another's is

25

laid down in the Bible as well as being the just punishment for the crime.

This does not have to be only for what is called 'first degree murder'. Any killing or even violence against the person, such as rape, could carry the death sentence. Dare I suggest that if people are killed by a drunken driver then the death sentence should also be available as a punishment? It would certainly concentrate the senses about drinking and driving.

Notice I say that the death sentence should be available. In many, if not most of the cases, some lesser punishment would be imposed. But the death penalty would be there as a possibility and, obviously, in some cases would be used. In a separate chapter I give some hypothetical cases and what, I believe, should be the just punishment.

There should then be a broad second category, in fact right across the entire spectrum of crime for which imprisonment could be the correct punishment. In other words, if you commit a horrendous murder the punishment could be imprisonment for a given number of years or even life, which should literally mean until you die. Or if you fail to pay a fine which is due then imprisonment again could be the answer. I have to say at this point that in both of the illustrations I have used I don't believe imprisonment to be the answer but it should be available as a punishment for any crime, however large or small, however serious or minuscule.

The third category is the fine, with no limit on the amount. Again, this would be up to the judge or judges or even the jury to determine. In today's climate there appear to be some strange amounts imposed, at both ends of the scale.

There are, of course, many other punishments that could be

used such as corporal punishment, electronic tagging or working to pay off debts, but for the moment I will confine myself to the three categories I have mentioned.

Then there is the whole question of age and length of time between the crime and the apprehension of the criminal.

I believe there should be no upper or lower age limit of non-responsibility. Because there is at the moment, the judges are hampered in their judgement and even in the right to charge an individual and bring him or her to court.

At the lower age level does this mean that a baby can be legally responsible for its actions? Of course not! But where should this legal age begin? At the moment it begins for some things at eighteen, for others at sixteen and for others even younger. But crimes and other misdemeanours are committed by children of all ages.

Should legal responsibility begin at eighteen? At seventeen? At sixteen? At fifteen? At fourteen? At thirteen? We all know that teenagers are capable of doing wrong. Should it go any lower? Down to twelve? Down to eleven? Down to ten? Down to nine? Where is the correct age for it to begin?

By doing away with the lower legal age limit you allow the judiciary and the courts and the police to exercise their discretion as to whether a minor should be brought to court or not. Of course you can't charge babies of one or two years of age but at what age can you charge them? By doing away with this lower age legality the guardians of our legal system are not hampered by this present legal requirement.

At the other end of the age scale what about people in their eighties who are apprehended late in life because of crimes they have committed earlier? Several of these have come to light in

27

recent days in connection with alleged atrocities committed during the Second World War. Should we prosecute them or, because they are old and possibly frail, forget it? Again, each case should be dealt with on its merits and if the evidence is there then the person should be charged and if found guilty, punished.

Right to Defend Oneself

What has the Bible got to say about this?

In the Sermon on the Mount Jesus said, ' "You have heard that it was said, an eye for an eye and a tooth for a tooth. But I say to you, do not resist one who is evil. But if anyone strikes you on the right cheek, turn to him the other also." ' (Matthew 5 v 38-39 RSV).

What Jesus is showing here is how the Believer should respond to personal injury. He is not discussing the responsibility of a government to maintain Law and Order. If Jesus had been advocating non-punishment of a criminal offence the Pharisees would have had him up in front of the Roman authorities immediately and he would have had no further opportunity to do the work that God had given him to do. Jesus is not discussing here the obligation of a government to maintain Law and Order.

Many people, theologians included, quote these verses for the pacifist cause whether in defence of an individual or a country. That is not their meaning but they are to show the Believer that he is not to exact personal revenge, even through the Courts.

Revenge, however, is not the same as Punishment.

When the daughter of Gordon Wilson was killed by an I.R.A. bomb in Enniskillen he said that he forgave them and didn't want revenge. That is not to say that the perpetrators of this crime should not have been brought to justice if they had been caught.

Revenge and Punishment are two different things. If they are not then there is no point whatsoever in ever trying to catch a criminal and the Bible never advocates this course of action.

When Jesus told the Parable of the Good Samaritan it was about a man who was travelling on the road from Jerusalem to Jericho, a dangerous road for anyone going that way. He fell among robbers who stripped him and beat him up and left him half dead. Now the Parable illustrates the goodness of the Samaritan over against the Levite and the Priest who should have done what the Samaritan did. We are not told what might have happened if there had been as many as or more travellers than there were robbers. Would they have put up resistance? We can't know, of course, because that's not what this Parable is about.

When Jesus is talking about his second coming to earth he illustrates this by saying that if a householder had known in what part of the night a thief was coming then he would have watched and would not have allowed his house to be broken into. (Matthew 24 v 43). Again the illustration does not state whether this would have been by diplomatic persuasion or whether force would have been used. Common sense dictates that argument would not have been sufficient.

The New Testament gives no examples of defence of one's property against robbers other than by implication and in any case that is not what the New Testament is about. It is about the coming of the Messiah, Jesus, into a sinful world, and going about for three years proclaiming the Gospel of repentance for sin and showing people what they have to do to return to a right relationship with God that was broken in the Garden of Eden right back at the beginning of creation. It tells about his birth, his upbringing, his death and crucifixion and his resurrection and ascension and the coming of God's Holy Spirit at Pentecost.

At the same time Jesus said, right at the beginning of his ministry, that he had come to fulfil the Law and not do away with it and that included the right to defend one's property as well as one's country.

It was that right that led to the Second World War as well as the defence of the Falkland Islands. When diplomacy was of no avail then action had to be taken to prevent evil from taking its course.

Anything Goes

We are living in an age of moral decay and that is even being quoted by people in authority as well as ordinary people. It is what people like Mary Whitehouse have been saying for over twenty five years and it is only now when horrendous crimes are being committed, so it seems, almost on a daily basis, that there is a public outcry that something must be done about it. What has brought it to a head was the terrible massacre of the children and their teacher by Thomas Hamilton at Dunblane Primary School.

Although I understand perfectly the outcry against weapons of destruction such as guns I believe that was only the means by which this tragedy was perpetrated and does not tackle the cause as to why it was carried out. I suspect there are many more 'Dunblanes' waiting to happen and the banning of guns legally held won't stop them happening unless the root causes are dug out. In Thomas Hamilton's case it would appear to be his unhealthy interest in young boys based on his addiction to pornography.

So the answer is not to get rid of the guns but to get rid of pornography. I would go so far as to say that if the writers and distributors of this filth could be apprehended then they should be standing in a court of law charged with the same offences as Thomas Hamilton would have been charged with if he had survived the killings. Further even than that, I believe the sentence that would have been imposed on Thomas Hamilton should be the one imposed on the pornographers. Capital punishment? Why not?

Jesus, when talking about the Kingdom of Heaven, put a child in the middle of the disciples and told them that '"whoever causes one of these little ones who believe in me to sin it would be better for him to have a great millstone fastened round his neck and to be drowned in the depth of the sea."' (Matthew 18 v 6 RSV). Not too much of the gentle Jesus meek and mild there! Would it be going too far to say that Jesus was here advocating Capital Punishment for anyone who led children astray? What would he have advocated for their wholesale murder? Remember God brought in Capital Punishment for disobedience right at the beginning of creation when Adam and Eve disobeyed God's command not to eat of the tree of the knowledge of good and evil. No, they were not killed immediately but death came into human creation right at the very beginning when it was not God's original intention that man should ever die. He would have found another way to take him into His eternal presence other than through the process of death.

And yet we have films being produced that portray violent sex and pornography and the writers and producers claiming that their 'art' is not allowed free expression. What utter arrogance!

Let's have a look if censorship was never exercised. In fact, I believe we are reaping the results today of a very lax censorship.

So now anything goes. But if people want censorship to go then have they really thought through the implications of this? It wouldn't just mean the abolition of censorship on films but the abolition of censorship on anything. In other words the Law would no longer be in existence and we could do exactly what we liked. We would have perfect freedom. More freedom than Adam and Eve because they were forbidden to do just one thing. We would not be forbidden to do anything. We should be perfectly happy but in fact the very opposite would be the case. It is in obedience that freedom can be found.

The problem would be there would be a problem. Other people! They might not agree with us. They might not want to go along with everything we wanted to do. They might want to kill us because they did not agree with the decisions we were making. And because censorship has gone there would be nothing to stop them doing just that. Because there were no laws there would be no punishment, no comeback, no responsibility. What on earth could we do about it? We would have to defend ourselves. We would have to join with like-minded people and set up some sort of defence. We would, heaven forbid(!), have to make some laws. We would have to have some kind of censorship preventing people from harming us.

If not, society would descend into anarchy.

And this is exactly the position we are rapidly heading towards today unless we bring in laws that are going to prevent people carrying out these dreadful atrocities.

> What causes wars, and what causes fightings among you? Is it not your passions that are at war in your members? You desire and do not have; so you kill. And you covet and cannot obtain; so you fight and wage war. You do not have, because you do not ask. You ask and do not receive, because you ask wrongly, to spend it on your passions. (James 4 v 1-3 RSV).

Where does all the trouble originate? It originates in the mind. When Adolf Hitler planned to rule the world it was in his mind that he conceived the plan, then he put it into action.

When Thomas Hamilton thought about killing the children in Dunblane it was in his mind that he conceived the plan and then he put it into action.

When we carry out any task it is in our minds that the germ has originated. And pornography feeds the basest instincts that are in man and it leads to many of the sexual crimes that are committed.

Forget the banning of weapons of destruction; they can never be uninvented. Concentrate on the banning of material that depraves and warps the mind. That's where all the problems arise and will arise in the future.

Anything goes? If it does we are heading down the road of anarchy and worse. We need to return, not to Victorian values, but to the values laid down in the Bible.

Remedies

There's a way back to God from the dark paths of sin;
There's a way that is open and you can go in.
At Calvary's cross is where you begin,
When you come as a sinner to Jesus.

So ran the chorus some of us learned as youngsters.

So simple in its message, so deep in its theology, so difficult to carry out.

We have all sinned. That's the first admission we have to make or we don't even get to the starting line. 'If we say we have no sin, we deceive ourselves, and the truth is not in us. If we confess our sins, he is faithful and just, and will forgive our sins and cleanse us from all unrighteousness. If we say we have not sinned, we make him a liar, and his word is not in us.' (1 John 1 v 8-10 RSV).

We need to read and follow the 'Roman' road as found in the New Testament book of Romans that Paul wrote to the Romans when he was at Corinth.

'As it is written, none is righteous, no not one, since all have sinned and fall short of the glory of God.' (Romans 3 v 10 & 23 RSV).

'Therefore as sin came into the world through one man and death through sin, and so death spread to all men because all men sinned ... For the wages of sin is death, but the free gift of God is eternal life in Christ Jesus our Lord.' (Romans 5 v 12 & 6 v 23 RSV).

'But God shows His love for us in that while we were yet sinners Christ died for us, because if you confess with your lips that Jesus is Lord and believe in your heart that God raised him from the dead, you will be saved. For everyone who calls upon the name of the Lord will be saved.' (Romans 5 v 8, 10 v 9 & 13 RSV).

This is what the Christian message is all about. This is the Good News of the Gospel. There is no other way.

The Bible is not a book about how good everyone was. It is in fact almost the opposite. It is a book about how the people quite often disobeyed God and God had to deal with them to bring them back to the way He wanted them to go.

It is a history of God's dealing with man through His people.

The people God used were not super human beings. They were fallible human beings just like ourselves.

The Old Testament contains books that show how God was dealing with His chosen people the Jews, known as the Israelites or Hebrews on other occasions. He often used individuals such as Noah, Abraham, Moses and others to bring the people back to the way He wanted them to go because, left on their own, they would do what they thought was right in their eyes. Not much of a different story to that which we find in the year 1999.

The New Testament contains the story of God's final revelation of Himself in Jesus Christ, His Son.

After the stories of his birth we don't hear much more until the announcement of his coming is made by John the Baptist.

For three years Jesus taught, preached and healed in the region of Judea, Samaria and Galilee. He chose and taught twelve disciples, one of whom betrayed him, to carry on his work when he had left this earth.

He was loved by the people he helped but hated by the Pharisees, the Jewish leaders, because he showed them up to be hypocrites. So much so that their only desire was to get rid of him by putting him to death. This they were unable to do at first because they were subject to the Law of the Romans who were the enemy occupying their land at this time.

It was only when Judas agreed to betray Jesus that they were able to take him into custody and falsely accuse him of blasphemy.

The Roman Governor, Pontius Pilate, had to make a decision about what to do with Jesus although he admitted that he could find no fault in him and wanted to release him. Because he wanted to keep in with the Pharisees he eventually handed Jesus over to the Roman authorities to be crucified, which was the Roman method of Capital Punishment.

Jesus was buried in a cave which belonged to a man by the name of Joseph who came from Arimathea. On the third day after his crucifixion God raised Jesus from the dead and he was seen by a large number of witnesses including his disciples who had not been expecting this outcome. There were more witnesses to the Resurrection of Jesus than are needed in a court of law to convict a person of a crime.

Why did Jesus have to die? Could not God have found another way?

The answer to that is no. Why?

Because of man's sin. Why?

Because sin separates man from God. Why?

Because God is Holy and man is sinful and that which is holy and that which is sinful cannot meet and mix. Why?

Because the Holiness of God would burn up that which is sinful and man would never be able to get into His presence.

So God had to find a way to bring man back into a close

relationship with Himself and the only way to do this was to provide a sacrifice that was without sin or blemish. The only way He could do this was through His Son, Jesus Christ.

Jesus took upon himself the sin of the world and at the cross at Calvary he was made sin for our sakes so that all who believe in him will not die but have eternal life.

So will everyone be saved in the end? Will everyone be in heaven? And if not why not?

Remember God is not only a God of Love but a God of Judgement as well. A God of perfect Love and a God of perfect Judgement.

' "For God so loved the world that He gave His only Son, that whoever believes in him should not perish but have eternal life." ' (John 3 v 16 RSV).

And it's the 'whoever' that is so important.

No one is compelled to accept Jesus Christ as his or her Lord and Saviour but if we have the knowledge that the only way to have eternal life with God in Eternity is to believe that Jesus is the Way to Him then we cannot complain if, having rejected the way God has provided, we find ourselves in Eternity and not in the presence of God. In other words we will be in Hell.

If you are going on a journey by car and you want to get to a certain destination and you either ignore the signposts telling you which direction you have to take or deliberately take the opposite way, then you can hardly complain when you fail to arrive at the place you wanted to go to.

You may even have taken a road map with you but you decide you know the way yourself without any reference to the experts who have put the map together. If you do this you are a fool.

In a similar way the Bible is our road map through the journey of life. Most people, so the statistics tell us, possess a copy in their house somewhere. If it is only propping up our furniture instead of being read and studied how can we complain when we discover, sometimes too late, that we are heading in the wrong direction and our ultimate journey's end is Hell?

What and where is Hell?

Hell is where God isn't and the Devil, Satan, is.

Hell, I believe, is where we will be able to see God but be unable to be near Him.

Hell will be an unending torment of the mind knowing that the decision we took whilst on earth not to accept Jesus as our Lord and Saviour has an eternal outcome.

Jesus said it is a place of eternal punishment. ' "And they will go away into eternal punishment, but the righteous into eternal life." ' (Matthew 25 v 46 RSV).

I believe the eternal world is in a spiritual dimension about which we know very little other than what is stated in the Bible.

We know that Jesus, after God raised him from the dead, was no longer bound by the limitations of our human existence. He could come and go as he pleased. His was now a spiritual body as ours will be in eternity.

What is certain is that it will be an exciting place to be without all the physical disabilities and frustrations that we have to undergo here on earth. And there will be no crime.

John, in his book of Revelation writes, 'God will wipe away every tear from their eyes, and death shall be no more, neither shall there be mourning nor crying nor pain any more, for the former things have passed away.' (Revelation 21 v 4 RSV).

We will, in fact, be back to the Paradise on earth that God had created for Adam and Eve in the garden of Eden but this time it will be for Eternity.

What can we do about it now in our own country?

It all comes back to these two words 'Obedience' and 'Punishment'.

If we obey the Law of the Land we do not get into trouble.

If we disobey the Law of the Land and are not found out we do not get into trouble.

Well, maybe not with the Law, but what about our consciences? If our consciences have been seared so much then even they are not a safety barrier. And if that happens what hope is there? With everyone doing what they consider to be right in their own eyes and not being reprimanded we are in a state of anarchy especially if what people are doing is evil and they think it is good.

In a Democracy we have to live with each other in a civilized way. If we don't then we are subject to the Laws of the Land and if we break those laws then we are liable to punishment. All of that would be accepted by most right-minded people, Christian or not. What is in dispute is what constitutes breaking the law and what punishments should be meted out if laws are broken.

For this we need again to go back to the Bible.

The Bible says that we are to be subject to the Law of the Land.

When the Pharisees wanted to trick Jesus into disobeying the Roman Law they thought they had him cornered regarding the payment of taxes. They said,

"Teacher, we know that you are true, and teach the way of God truthfully, and care for no man; for you do not regard the

39

position of men. Tell us, then, what you think. Is it lawful to pay taxes to Caesar, or not?" But Jesus, aware of their malice, said, "Why put me to the test, you hypocrites? Show me the money for the tax." And they brought him a coin. And Jesus said to them, "Whose likeness and inscription is this?" They said, "Caesar's." Then he said to them, "Render therefore to Caesar the things that are Caesar's, and to God the things that are God's." When they heard it, they marvelled; and they left him and went away. (Matthew 22 v 16-22 RSV).

In other words, even Jesus was subject to the Roman Law providing it did not contradict the Law of God.

Jesus was without sin and lived a perfect life in accordance with God's will and so was able to become the perfect sacrifice when he laid down his life on the cross at Calvary.

We are not perfect; we have all sinned and, I suspect, most of us have committed crimes, albeit only ones relating to taxes! The punishment for evading taxes might be a fine or it might be imprisonment. To my mind the correct punishment for financial crimes should be where the criminal has the opportunity to make restitution for what he has done. Like Zacchaeus, to restore it fourfold? (Luke 19 v 8 RSV). What is the point of putting non-dangerous people in our overcrowded prisons? In fact, I believe that prisons should be as empty as possible but that is a subject of another chapter.

In this book I am mainly concerned with crimes which make people afraid. Afraid to walk out in our towns on a Saturday afternoon; afraid to go out after dark; afraid to even go out in the car alone at night; afraid to walk under a subway; afraid to go for a walk in the woods; afraid to walk down a country lane; afraid to walk across a field; afraid to go out and leave the house unoccupied; afraid to stay in the house alone. These are the fears that have to be addressed by our politicians and lawmakers and when crimes happen where any of these situations are involved then the punishment has to fit the crime or the Government and the Law lose all credibility.

In another chapter I give some hypothetical situations based on real cases that have appeared in the newspapers and the punishments which I believe to be the just ones.

Hypothetical Cases and Suggested Punishments

In all of the cases illustrated here I am assuming the evidence for the crime is overwhelming. If the only evidence is the confession of the person concerned, whether under questioning by police officers or by voluntarily walking into a police station and confessing, then the sentence, if the accused is found to be guilty, should be different.

All names of people are entirely fictitious and any resemblance to anyone, alive or dead, is entirely coincidental.

Boy Murdered by the Side of a Canal

John Collins had taken his fishing rod and line along to the Manston Canal as he usually did on a Saturday afternoon. It wasn't for him to go to see the local soccer team with all of his mates. He got on well with all of his friends but he just wasn't interested in going to watch football matches.

He used to take his lunch with him and several of his mates used to see him as they walked by on the towpath on their way to watch Barchester United. Quite often he would still be there when they were making their way home except in the depth of winter when it got dark rather early.

On the occasion in question they had passed John on their way to see the football match at about 2 o'clock when he had just caught a fish. They made a comment to him and said they might see him again on the way home.

As it happened the match had to be abandoned because the floodlights failed when they were switched on at half time and despite trying to get them to work for over half an hour it was finally decided that the match would have to be replayed.

Because of this they left the ground fifteen minutes early.

As they came round the bend in the towpath of the canal about two hundred yards from where John was fishing they saw and heard an argument. They saw a man, Fred Hutchins, hit John over the head with a blunt instrument and he fell into the water.

All four of them ran as fast as they could to where they had seen John fall in and two of them, Paul Snow and Ian Mitchell, jumped into the canal and managed to get John on to the bank.

Meanwhile George Carpenter and Peter Talbot chased after the man whom they had seen hit John over the head.

Although he had about 150 yards start George and Peter were very fit and soon gained on him. Fred Hutchins, however, might still have got away from them if he hadn't looked back to see how far away they were and then tripped over a stone which was on the towpath.

Just as Fred was getting to his feet they pounced on him and knocked him unconscious. George Carpenter ran to a nearby house and got the occupants to phone for the police and ambulance.

Back at the spot where Paul Snow and Ian Mitchell had got John Collins on to the canal bank they could see that he was in a bad way.

The police and ambulance came very quickly but they were unable to do anything for John Collins as he was already dead.

After they had listened to the story of the four friends of John Collins they took Fred Hutchins away in the police van.

At the subsequent trial it transpired that Fred Hutchins had been watching John Collins from a hiding-place on the canal bank and had looked for an opportunity to find him on his own. He had seen that every Saturday afternoon the canal bank was deserted except for John and he had taken the opportunity to approach John when he believed they would not be disturbed by anyone else.

Because the floodlights had failed at the local football match John Collins' friends returned along the towpath much earlier than Fred Hutchins had expected and he was caught in the act of hitting him over the head and pushing him into the canal.

At the trial there was irrefutable evidence that Fred Hutchins had committed the murder, not only because he had been seen by four reliable witnesses but also because his finger-prints had been found on the blunt instrument he used to hit John Collins with and which was found lying on the towpath where he had committed the crime and which, because of being seen by John Collins' four friends, he had left there when he had tried to escape from them.

The jury, unanimously, found Fred Hutchins guilty of murder.

The judge, when passing sentence, revealed that Fred Hutchins had a history of violence and sexual assault against boys. The sentence was capital punishment.

Gang Rape of Sixteen Year Old

Julie Roberts had been waiting at a bus stop in a country lane at about 11 o'clock in the morning having just been to visit her aunt who had not been very well.

Four youths pulled up in a car and abducted her and took her to an isolated barn where all four of them took it in turns to rape her despite her pleas to be left alone.

They also subjected her to all kinds of humiliation.

Her screams, however, had attracted the attention of a farmer who was out hunting for rabbits and carrying a shotgun. He entered the barn and caught them in the act of assault. He ordered them to leave the girl alone and got out his mobile phone in order to contact the police. At this one of the youths ran towards him but the farmer, John Edwards, raised his shotgun and fired. The youth fell to the ground and the other three youths cowered, pleading not to be shot.

The farmer managed to contact the police and asked for the ambulance service as well.

The farmer explained what had happened and the three youths were taken away to the police station for questioning, the youth who was shot was taken to the local hospital where he later on died from his wounds and the girl, Julie Roberts, was also taken to the hospital, where she was comforted and helped by a female police officer and hospital staff.

At the trial the testimony of the farmer was corroborated by

Julie Roberts and there was medical evidence to support the fact that she had been continually raped.

The jury, unanimously, found the three youths guilty of rape. They exonerated the farmer from any criminal liability and praised him for his public-spirited action.

The judge, when summing up, reported that all four of the youths had a history of petty crime and had been suspected of rape previously but the evidence had been insufficient. On this occasion there was sufficient evidence, as the jury agreed, to convict them and the judge sentenced all three of them with capital punishment.

Wife Kills Husband with Hammer

Jacqueline Baker and her husband Herbert Baker had been married for twenty seven years. They lived in a detached house in a suburb of London.

They had two children, Robert and Jean, both of whom were now married and had emigrated, Robert to Canada and Jean to Australia.

Herbert Baker had a reputation for being a womanizer and this had caused friction between him and his wife for a number of years but Jacqueline had stayed with her husband for the sake of the children; but now that they were married and had left home things had gone from bad to worse.

As well as being unfaithful to his wife, Herbert Baker had taken to coming home drunk on numerous occasions and beating his wife.

This had gone on for four months until Jacqueline Baker

could stand it no longer and she decided to tell her husband that she was going to leave him.

When she told him he got into another rage and started to hit her. Jacqueline picked up a hammer, which happened to be lying on the draining board, and hit her husband over the head. He collapsed in a heap on the floor.

Jacqueline Baker phoned the police and the ambulance services who came quickly. Herbert Baker was taken to the nearest hospital, where he was pronounced dead on arrival, killed by a blow to the temple.

Jacqueline was taken to the police station where she was questioned about her husband's death. She was charged with his murder and sent for trial.

At the trial she admitted hitting her husband over the head and all the details of her unhappy married life came out into the open.

Robert Baker and Jean Hunter, her two children, returned to England to support their mother and they also testified to the fact that their father had been unfaithful and that he had a violent temper.

The jury, although they acknowledged the fact that Jacqueline Baker had killed her violent husband, found her not guilty and recommended that she be released immediately as she had suffered enough already and had been pushed to the end of her tether because what she had done was totally out of character as she was a non-violent person as both of her children and other witnesses had testified.

The judge took the recommendation of the jury and she was released.

Mugging Goes Wrong

Peter Smith was walking along the pavement of a quiet road on his way back from going to the Bank when he became aware that a car had pulled up alongside him.

His first thought was that someone was going to ask for directions when three men jumped out of the car and demanded that he hand over the money that they had seen him get from the cash dispenser outside the Midland Bank.

Instantaneously he jumped into action as he was a trained judo expert. He kneed the first man in the groin who fell back and cracked his head on the pavement and at almost the same time he banged the heads together of the other two men who also fell down and hit their heads on the pavement.

The engine of the car was still running so Peter Smith turned off the ignition and was just about to go into the nearest house to ask for help when a middle-aged woman came running out and said she had seen all that had taken place as she was cleaning the windows in one of her upstairs bedrooms.

Peter Smith asked her to phone for the police and an ambulance.

When they came, the ambulance men could see that all three of the muggers were dead and the coroner confirmed that one had died from hitting his head on the pavement following a heavy fall whilst the two others had died from brain damage when their heads were banged together.

The police took a statement from Peter Smith and from Hetty White, the woman who had witnessed the incident from beginning to end, and no charge was brought against Peter Smith.

Burglary Causes Elderly Woman to Die

Kurt Walstaff broke into the semi-detached house by forcing a window at the rear of the building. He had searched all the rooms downstairs and taken the television and video recorder outside to take away in his van which was parked in a dimly lit service road at the rear of the house. He was making his way upstairs thinking that the house was empty when an elderly woman, May Jenkins, appeared at the top of the stairs barring his way. He went to push past her and as he did so he knocked her off her balance and she toppled down the stairs right to the bottom and fractured her skull.

At this Kurt Walstaff took fright and ran out of the front door in panic.

As it happened, a neighbour who lived opposite to May Jenkins, a Mrs Mary Bickerstaff, had turned off her light just before going to bed when she had noticed a light from what she thought was a torch in the house of May Jenkins. Knowing that May Jenkins always switched on the light if she got up in the night Mary Bickerstaff phoned the police who came just as Kurt Walstaff was running out of the front door.

Kurt Walstaff ran straight into the arms of the two policemen who had come to investigate. They took him back inside the house where they discovered the body of May Jenkins. They phoned for an ambulance but when they arrived May Jenkins was pronounced as being dead.

Kurt Walstaff was charged with murder as this was a risk he took when he broke into anyone's house knowing that if anyone was killed or even died of a heart attack because of the stress caused by the burglary then the punishment could be a capital one.

The jury came to a unanimous conclusion that May Jenkins died as a direct result of the breaking and entering and Kurt Walstaff was sentenced with capital punishment.

Armed Robbery Foiled

It was 10.30 in the morning when a gang of three armed robbers with masks over their faces came into the Midland Bank in Tangier Street and demanded money from the cashier. Instructions from Head Office were to hand over any money available in order to save the possibility of being shot. This the cashier did but at the same time pressed an alarm bell which went straight to the local police station without making any noise within the Bank so the robbers were not aware that the alarm had been raised.

Five thousand pounds had been handed over and the robbers were making their way back to their stolen car when they were ambushed by six armed policemen. The getaway driver of the stolen car had already been arrested and disarmed.

Seeing the policemen as they emerged from the Bank they attempted to shoot their way out of trouble but when one of their number was shot dead and another was wounded the third robber surrendered.

The three remaining robbers, which included the driver of the getaway car, who were still alive were all charged with armed robbery.

The jury, unanimously, found them all guilty of armed robbery.

The judge sentenced all three of them with capital punishment.

House Burgled Whilst Owners Were Away on Holiday

Philip and Georgina Prendergast had saved up for a special holiday for years so they went away in August to Canada for three weeks to celebrate their Ruby Wedding. They had always wanted to visit Canada and in particular the Rockies and Victoria. They flew to Vancouver and hired a car to travel around in British Columbia and Alberta.

They had a marvellous time, the weather was perfect, they saw a great deal of wild life and they had taken a lot of pictures both on slides and on prints.

Imagine their feelings when they returned to their detached house in the Chilterns to discover that they had been burgled. Entry had been by a fanlight window at the back of the house and everything had been turned upside down. Every conceivable drawer had been taken out and clothing strewed everywhere.

All Georgina Prendergast's valuables had been taken and many of the valuable antiques that were in the lounge and dining-room had been wantonly smashed.

Philip Prendergast called the police and tried to comfort his wife who was, quite understandably, very upset.

The police suspected two youths, Ben Fleming and Gerald Ponting, to be the culprits as they knew they were responsible for many of the burglaries that had taken place in the area over the last year but they had never been able to prove that they had committed these crimes.

However, on this occasion, the burglars had been careless enough to leave fingerprints on several of the broken antique items. These were enough to prove that both Ben Fleming and Gerald Ponting had been responsible for this particular burglary and the police went ahead and prosecuted them.

The jury, unanimously, found both of them guilty of this burglary and they asked for ten other burglaries to be taken into consideration.

The judge handed out a sentence of twenty years in prison with remission possible if they were able to pay off the amount they had stolen or ruined in the Prendergast home.

Punishment as a Deterrent

I would always argue punishment as a punishment and not as a deterrent. As far as I can see the Bible never states that if someone is punished then others will be deterred from following suit. Undoubtedly the Roman punishment of crucifixion served as a deterrent but that was what the Romans believed and not what God laid down as the reason for punishment. Punishment in the Bible was always for wrongdoing.

It has frequently been stated that the greatest deterrent to crime is the thought of being caught. I don't believe this to be the case at all. For all of the above hypothetical cases, barring one, that I have used as illustrations I believe that they would not have happened if the criminals concerned had thought there was the possibility that they would lose their lives if caught or spend so many years in prison. However, criminals today are not deterred by the thought of being caught or even the punishment that would be meted out because the punishment in so many cases doesn't fit the crime. In my opinion sentences are far too lenient, prisons appear to be more like leisure centres and many offenders commit crimes again once they are released.

Even if, and I don't believe there is an if, capital punishment doesn't deter others from committing the same crime, at least those who have been convicted of capital offences won't be able to repeat their criminal activities.

As a side effect, and I wouldn't argue this as a reason for capital punishment, the State is saved considerable sums of money by not having to keep violent criminals in prison.

'The thought of capital punishment didn't deter the woman who killed her violent husband,' I can hear being voiced. True, but she was found to be not guilty of murder and was released. Now I wouldn't like to give licence to every woman to do away with a husband she didn't get on with but there must be sympathy with those women who have been abused by their husbands and have reached the end of their tether. In a moment of temper or of losing control of course they are not going to think about the consequences. Each case must be taken on its merit but in most of the cases the wife concerned is no danger to the public at large, is unlikely ever to do the same thing again, so what is the point of incarcerating her in a prison for any length of time?

One of the most distressing things for people to find out when they return from a shopping trip or an evening out is to discover that their house has been burgled.

Burglary is an invasion of another person's territory and needs to be dealt with in a much more stringent manner.

If anyone has been injured or killed during the course of a burglary then the ultimate penalty must be available for the judge to apply.

In the case of burglary where the house is unoccupied then two courses may be open; one, the burglar is given a reasonable amount of time to repay the amount stolen plus compensation for inconvenience and harassment or two, imprisonment for a long time for persistent burglars.

In financial scandals, the thought of having to repay anything up to four times the amount back might well deter some people from committing the felony in the first place. Now if the amount involved runs into hundreds of thousands or even greater amounts then imprisonment may be the only answer, but the time to be served should be long enough to deter others from doing the same crime.

Bands of Punishment

As I have already indicated previously I believe there should be, broadly speaking, three bands of punishment.

The first is capital punishment. Where a crime is committed and this results in death or injury to a person then capital punishment should be available as an option. Even if it is rarely or never used it stands there as a measure of value of a human being's worth.

The second, and broadest band, would be imprisonment. This would be available for any crime committed from murder down to book crimes. As far as possible there should be fewer and fewer people being put in prison and in the main, only those who are a danger to society at large or if there is no other

OBEDIENCE

possible way to pay back the person wronged then imprisonment it would have to be.

The third band would be by way of a fine or repayment to
the person wronged up to, say, four times the value of the
money embezzled or stolen.

There is therefore no way that anyone who has committed a
murder would be fined and no way that anyone who has stolen
money would be put to death.

Ideally every punishment should fit the crime. Perfect
justice, which is what is meant when the Bible talks about 'an
eye for an eye and a tooth for a tooth'.

Would it be asking too much these days to feed all the
information into a computer and let it come up with the just
punishment! A human being, or human beings, however,
should have the last word!

Punishment: Revenge or Deterrent?

If we follow the cases that are brought up in court, whether
they are violent attacks on the individual or complicated
financial scandals, when the judge hands out the sentence,
assuming the person prosecuted is found guilty, we often hear
the relatives and friends of the plaintiff complaining that the
sentence is insufficient or the relatives and friends of the
accused believing that the sentence is too harsh.

When the case is argued for and against capital punishment,
one of the arguments heard is that capital punishment is really
capital revenge.

If you can recall your Algebra from your days back in school

54

you will remember that anything on the left of the equation is always equal to anything on the right of the equation.

In that case Capital Punishment = Capital Revenge.

If we remove the words that appear on both sides of the equation then we are left with the following:-

Punishment = Revenge

If that is the case and we are merely trying to get our own back on the criminal then that is wrong. In fact God has stated that '"Vengeance is mine, I will repay, says the Lord."' (Romans 12 v 19 RSV).

So if revenge is wrong and punishment equals revenge then no one should be punished. We are back to the state of anarchy.

I imagine that most people would not accept that revenge and punishment are exactly the same and therefore capital revenge and capital punishment are not exactly the same.

So, by a simple equation, we have proved that because punishment is not the same as revenge then capital punishment is not the same as capital revenge.

While the Bible states that revenge is wrong it also states that punishment is necessary. If offenders are not caught and suitably punished then the crime rate goes up and people live in fear even in their own homes, particularly the elderly and women.

Both main political parties claim to be the party of Law and Order but all the time crimes are being committed and fewer offenders are being brought to justice and even when they are apprehended and sentenced the punishment often seems not to fit the crime.

A report in the *Daily Telegraph* (4.1.97) states that the number of violent and sexual offenders brought to justice has fallen despite rising crime figures. The report was a survey made by Labour. To make a political point Jack Straw said that violent offenders are almost three times more likely to get away with their crimes than when the Tories took office.

No doubt the Conservatives would refute this and claim that Labour have done, and would do, no better.

Between 1980 and 1995 the number of recorded violent offences went up by 137 per cent from 133,359 to 316,332. Yet convictions dropped by almost 15 per cent to 61,398.

Why?

All kinds of reasons are given for the increase in the crime rate, ranging from unemployment through bad social conditions to the breakdown of marriage and, no doubt, all of these have some part to play. But you might as well do a study of criminals and come up with the answer that more blue-eyed people commit murder than people with brown eyes! What does that prove? And what would be the suggested solution to the problem? Get the medical profession to find a way to eradicate people being born with blue eyes?

The mind boggles! And of course it wouldn't solve the problem.

Why not? Because the wrong question would have been asked and the wrong solution found.

So what is the answer to the rising crime rate?

Treatment

There is a body of opinion that believes that many criminals are not in need of punishment at all but are in need of treatment. If they receive the right treatment then their problems may be solved.

It could be that a trip to Disneyland in Florida may do away with all the inhibitions that a young thug has and on his return he can be rehabilitated into society.

The evidence that this would be the case is not borne out by the experiments that have taken place. After all, if you can get a free holiday in Florida because you have been involved in criminal activities then it would be to your advantage to offend again and get another free holiday in a game reserve in Kenya! In fact, you could arrange to see the world at the tax payer's expense merely by committing crimes.

Can you imagine an enterprising travel agent issuing a brochure aimed at attracting young offenders, with discounts for bad behaviour! Book your next year's vacation now!

Surely the answer is not to reward the criminal for his crime, which is what such treatment would be deemed to be by the law-abiding population, but to find a method which would ensure that the offender never wants to offend again.

So, every first offender should not be let off with a caution but undergo some punishment which would end up with him stating that he never wants to experience that again.

Just, but not cruel.

Sufficiently hard but not harsh.

This is more likely to have the desired effect than what must be seen as a reward for bad behaviour.

How much better it would be, however, if it never reached the stage where a young person's aggression appeared in public.

How can this be achieved?

Marriage Breakdown

All discipline should start in the home.

At what age?

From the moment a baby is born.

Even babies shouldn't be given everything they want, when they want.

Can you remember, if you are a parent, being woken up in the night and hearing the demand to be fed from your newly arrived offspring? The cry of a baby in the night affects all who are disturbed by it.

Of course you must do something about it then but there are times when the crying is just a temper tantrum and you need to discover the difference between a need and a want.

The 'I needs' have to be answered but the 'I wants' have to be dealt with in a different way. Not just when the offspring is a baby but throughout the rest of his life and that includes us as adults.

It is the 'I wants' that cause all the trouble.

Have you ever been in a supermarket when you've heard the plaintive cry from an infant that he 'wants' something? What is the answer given by the harassed parent, normally the mother?

It varies, of course. From the weak acquiescence that ensures that the request will come again and in quite a quick time, through the 'Not now, dear!' to the 'Wait till I get you home and then you're for it!' syndrome.

Bringing up a child, and in most cases this means children, is a full-time occupation, requiring two parents, a mother and a father. That is Biblical and how God intended it to be. The fact that it sometimes went wrong, even in Biblical times, is not God's fault, but the fault of the people concerned.

God created man in His own image. I suppose that God could have gone on creating men in His image but that was not the way He did it. He provided a human way for reproduction by creating a woman and giving her to the man He had already created. 'Then the man said, "This at last is bone of my bones and flesh of my flesh; she shall be called Woman, because she was taken out of Man." Therefore a man leaves his father and his mother and cleaves to his wife, and they become one flesh.' (Genesis 2 v 23-24 RSV).

We can see from this passage that marriage was instituted by God, not an arrangement by man, and it is to God's Word, the Bible, that we need to turn in order to show us how we should live. God gave Adam only one wife and the relationship was a heterosexual one.

There is no hint of any homosexual relationship sanctioned by God nor of a one-parent family relationship being the norm. It's when we deviate from that standard that we begin to cause difficulties for ourselves. Even within the two-parent, male and female, family relationship there can be problems that arise and that's when such a stable environment is invaluable. When that is not there the problems can be so much more difficult to overcome. Within that generalization there can always be exceptions.

Hence the increasing tendency for marriages to break down is causing many of the problems that might be associated with one-parent families in addition to second marriages where there must be the inevitable tensions caused by the new step-father or step-mother, normally the former.

If the average family have two children then this can take twenty years before they both leave home and sometimes longer. This means twenty years to establish care and control over them, twenty years to teach them right from wrong, twenty years to be together on discipline and twenty years, if coming from a Christian home, to teach them the truths of the Bible.

If this was the norm in every home I believe we would see an end to most of the crime that we experience in our country.

I don't know whether there has been a study on the background of all the criminals at any one time in the prisons of our land but my guess would be that there would be a very low percentage there who come from a two-parent, male and female, family.

If that is the case then we need to take very seriously indeed our attitude to marriage and to make it much harder for parents to abrogate their responsibilities.

As it stands at the moment I can only foresee that circumstances are going to deteriorate even further. Boys are not readily going to accept discipline from a man who is not their natural father. This can lead to violence in the home and the boy then running away and either ending up in care or sleeping rough on the streets, neither of which is satisfactory. If a girl is involved then there is always the possibility of sexual assault and the same problem of being taken into care or running away.

Why Jesus Came

Most people in this country, whether Christian or non-Christian, would admit that we have a problem with Law and Order.

The very fact that we lock up our houses when we go out, provide security locks for all our doors and windows, install a security and lighting system, belong to a neighbourhood watch group, buy a fierce-looking dog or put up a notice saying 'Beware of the cobras!' all indicate that we are not very secure when we leave our house for a holiday or even go out for the evening.

When we park our car we are encouraged to leave it under a light or put it in a secure and patrolled car park. We may also have a wheel-lock and an alarm system fixed to help deter theft. Various notices are stuck to the windows indicating that the car is fixed with tracking devices or the radio has a number code which means it can't be used if removed from the vehicle.

If we're out walking on our own, which increasing numbers of women in particular are no longer doing, even if accompanied by a dog, then we may be carrying a spray of some kind or a personal alarm in order to deter a possible attacker.

And these are only the tip of the iceberg where crime is concerned.

Humanity has gone wrong and we can't rectify the situation in our own strength. We need outside help.

And that's why Jesus came.

God had created a perfect world. Everything in it was good. Into this perfect world, this paradise, God placed man. Because it wasn't good for man to live alone God gave him woman as a companion and to keep His creation going, the means to procreate.

As we have seen, Adam and Eve were tempted by the Devil. They succumbed to his temptation and ate of the tree of knowledge of good and evil. Things could never be the same.

They had disobeyed God. The one thing He told them they should not do they did. Disobedience to God is called sin. They had of their own free will, through disobedience, alienated themselves from God. They were sent out from the Garden of Eden never to return.

Why did their disobedience alienate them from God?

Because God is Holy and that which is Holy cannot meet and mix with that which is sinful. The unholy part has to be cleansed before they can have fellowship again.

In the Gulf War Saddam Hussein released a large quantity of oil into the Gulf waters. These two liquids met but they did not mix. Before the water could be proclaimed pure once more the oil had to be dispersed by a cleansing agent. When this was done and finished the water was clean again.

Similarly, there has to be a cleansing before man can get back into a right relationship with God.

The rest of the Old Testament is really a history of God's dealings with a nation, the Jews (or Hebrews or Israelites as they were also known at various times).

The Jews kept on sinning and God kept on providing a way back to Himself.

At various times in the history of the Hebrew nation He raised up men such as Abraham, Joseph, Moses, David and the Prophets to lead His people in the way He wanted them to go.

Frequently a sacrifice was made because the people realised they had sinned and needed to seek forgiveness.

When God was preparing the Israelites for their escape from captivity in Egypt He told Moses to tell them to sacrifice a lamb which had to be pure, without any blemish. They were to take some of the blood and sprinkle it on the doorposts and the lintel of the houses where they were. It was the Lord's Passover. When the first-born in Egypt were killed, death did not come to those houses where the blood of the lamb had been sprinkled on the doorposts. Where the people had obeyed God in doing this God did not destroy them.

God wanted obedience. He wanted it then. He wants it now. We need it now.

From Egypt back to the Promised Land, God was preparing His people for the coming of the Messiah.

It had, however, to be at the right time, in the right place, among the right nation.

So it was to Mary and Joseph that Jesus, the Messiah, was born.

Christmas testifies to that fact.

Our dating system testifies to that fact, although when the calendar was fixed they misjudged the years so we probably celebrated the second millennium in 1996 without knowing it!

However, preparations for the year 2000 are going ahead regardless. But we always need to remember what we are remembering, namely the birth of Christ in Bethlehem.

Obviously the birth of Jesus is important but that was only the beginning.

We celebrate Christmas but large numbers of people have left out the person whose birthday we are remembering. That would be like celebrating the birthday of one of our children and not inviting him to the party!

The Gospels of Matthew and Luke tell us about the Christmas story when the Shepherds and later on the Wise Men came to visit Jesus in Bethlehem but we don't hear much more in the Bible about him except for one event in Jerusalem when he was twelve years old, until John the Baptist announces his coming by saying, '"Behold, the Lamb of God, who takes away the sin of the world."' (John 1 v 29 RSV).

Jesus himself said, '"The time is fulfilled, and the Kingdom of God is at hand; repent, and believe in the Gospel."' (Mark 1 v 15 RSV).

That was the message of Jesus then and that is the message of Jesus today.

Repent and believe.

That is the message that should be being proclaimed from the pulpit of every Christian Church but more than that it should be the message being proclaimed from other pulpits as well.

When Jesus preached in Judea and Galilee he preached from the mountain side, in the market place, by the Sea of Galilee. In fact, he preached wherever people were to be found.

Where are people to be found today?

Yes, they are still to be found in the market place or in the supermarkets but not very many are climbing mountains, although the effort might do them good and cut out the risk of heart attacks!

But most people are to be found in front of their television sets.

Statistics state that we watch on average several hours of television every day.

My guess is that in many homes the television is switched on in the evening, or even earlier, and not switched off until the last person turns in for the night.

The fact that programmes go on all through the night testifies to the fact that there must be some demand for it even then.

OBEDIENCE

I believe that if Jesus had come today he would have used the television screen as one of his pulpits.

His pulpits might have varied but his message would still be the same.

We need to confess our sin, our disobedience to the way that God wants us to live, just as Adam and Eve disobeyed God in the Garden of Eden.

But just as the Jewish leaders and many others rejected what Jesus had to say when he lived in Judea so I believe many would have rejected both his message and him today.

So what happened those two thousand years ago?

Jesus went to the cross and was crucified.

Why?

Because God was providing a way back to a relationship with Himself which was broken in the Garden of Eden and which we inherit as descendants of Adam. We are sinners by inheritance and sinners by our own actions. Either way we are cut off from fellowship with God and the only way back was for God to provide a way Himself. He did this by sending Jesus (the name means Saviour) to be that person.

Jesus himself said that he was the Way: ' "I am the way, and the truth, and the life; no one comes to the Father, but by me." ' (John 14 v 6 RSV).

Why was it necessary that Jesus had to die?

Because, as we have already seen, God is Holy, and that which is Holy cannot meet and mix with that which is sinful. There had to be a price that had to be paid. That price was the life of a person that was perfect and without any fault at all. The only person who fitted all these criteria was Jesus. He lived a life in perfect obedience to God, his Father.

65

In the sacrifice of his life on the cross, something which was perfect in every way was given as a means of our reconciliation with a Holy God. If we, being sinful, were to gaze on the face of God we would be burnt up by His holiness. We can only come into the presence of God through our belief in Jesus Christ as our Saviour and Lord.

It is what the Bible calls being born again.

That is what Jesus told Nicodemus when this Pharisee came to visit Jesus by night because he didn't want to be seen in the company of Jesus by his fellow Pharisees.

Jesus told him he had to be born again. It appears Nicodemus took notice of what Jesus said because he helped Joseph of Arimathea take down the body of Jesus from the cross after he had been crucified and place his body in the Garden tomb.

If God could have found another way to bring man back into a right relationship with Himself then He would have found it, but there was no other way. '"For God so loved the world that he gave his only Son, that whoever believes in him should not perish but have eternal life."' (John 3 v 16 RSV).

That's why Jesus came – to do his Father's will, which was to reconcile man with Himself.

Will all then be saved?

Will everyone be in Heaven?

To answer this we need to look again at what God says in His Book, the Bible.

Heaven

What is Heaven?
Heaven is a place where God is.
Heaven is a place where Jesus is.
Heaven is a place where the Holy Spirit is.
Heaven is a place where angels are.
Heaven is a place where there is no evil.
Heaven is a place where those who have trusted in Jesus Christ as Lord and Saviour are.
Heaven is a place where there is no evil.
Heaven is a place where there is no more parting.
Heaven is a place where there is no more sorrow.
Heaven is a place of Eternal Life.
Heaven is a place where we will be worshipping God.
Heaven is a place where we will have fellowship with each other.
Heaven is a place where we will have a new body.
And all of that can be found in the pages of the Bible.

We could imagine in our own minds so much more but all of that is enough to be going on with until that day when those who love the Lord will be with him for ever.

There are many other questions we would like to have answered while we are here on earth but we will have to wait until we are in Heaven before we get them.

The opening words of the Biblical books of Genesis and John indicate that right at the beginning God and Jesus existed. 'In the beginning God created the heavens and the earth.' (Genesis 1 v 1 RSV). 'In the beginning was the Word, and the Word was with God, and the Word was God.' (John 1 v 1 RSV).

Living in the place along with God and Jesus were angelic beings – angels.

Who created God? That is a question frequently asked and the answer is no one. God is not a created Being. God is the creator.

The verb 'created' and 'God' do not exist next to each other just like the verb 'fought' and 'bed' would not belong in a sentence 'I fought a bed.' They would not make sense. Neither does the sentence 'Who created God?'

That may be difficult for some people to accept but we accept the statement by faith.

Christianity is the Christian faith not the Christian proof.

A Christian's 'Text Book' is the Bible.

In its pages, both the Old Testament and the New Testament, we find God's revelation of Himself and His plan for mankind.

It tells us about Creation.

It tells us about the Fall, that is, how man disobeyed God and was separated from Him.

It tells us how God is concerned for His people, the Jews, and most of the Old Testament is His dealings with them, leading them out of captivity in Egypt, back to the Promised Land we now know as Israel and leading up to the coming of the promised Messiah.

The New Testament is about the coming of the Messiah, Jesus Christ; it's about the call of his disciples; it's about the teaching, preaching and healing that Jesus did while he was here on earth; it's about the missionary work carried out by the disciples; it includes the letters of Paul to the Churches that Paul started in Asia and it culminates in the Revelation to John on the Island of Patmos.

In these Books are to be found the way that God wants us to live our lives and because we have all fallen short of how God wants us to live, we need to find the way back into fellowship with Him through our trust in Jesus Christ as Lord and Saviour.

The Bible tells us how to do that: 'Now Jesus did many other signs in the presence of the disciples, which are not written in this book; but these are written that you may believe that Jesus is the Christ, the Son of God, and that believing you may have life in his name.' (John 20 v 30-31 RSV).

The life that is talked about here is spiritual life. Adam, by disobeying God in the Garden of Eden, brought death into the world, both physical death and spiritual death.

Jesus, by his death on the cross, has provided a way back into fellowship with God for all who believe in him as the Saviour.

Those who have accepted Jesus as their Saviour will not die spiritually but will be with God in Eternity in Heaven.

Physical death will always be with us but the soul will never die. Jesus taught that. At death there is not an eternity in heaven for the believers and annihilation for everyone else. Those who die having rejected the way provided by Jesus at the cross will not just cease to exist but will spend an eternity in Hell. We will look at this in another chapter.

How do we know all this?

How do we know anything?

After Jesus had risen from the dead he appeared to the women when they went to the Tomb to embalm his body. He appeared to Peter and John. He appeared to the disciples. He appeared to Paul on the road to Damascus. At one time he appeared to more than five hundred men.

The evidence of the Resurrection is overwhelming. There are

more witnesses to the fact that Jesus rose from the dead than are needed in a court of law in England to convict anyone of a crime.

The evidence of a witness or witnesses in a court of law is of supreme importance, of course.

On the evening of the day we now know as Easter Sunday Jesus appeared to the disciples and showed them his hands and his side. Thomas was not with them on this occasion and told them,

> "Unless I see in his hands the print of the nails, and place my finger in the mark of the nails, and place my hand in his side, I will not believe." Eight days later, his disciples were again in the house, and Thomas was with them. The doors were shut, but Jesus came and stood among them, and said, "Peace be with you." Then he said to Thomas, "Put your finger here, and see my hands; and put out your hand, and place it in my side; do not be faithless but believing." Thomas answered him, "My Lord and my God." Jesus said to him, "Have you believed because you have seen me? Blessed are those who have not seen and yet believe." (John 20 v 25-29 RSV).

That is faith. Trusting in the word of someone they have not seen. Most Christians alive today have not seen Jesus in the flesh but we believe all that he said as recorded in the pages of the Bible.

Do you tell the truth always?

Do you believe others when they tell you anything?

Do you believe the secretary on the end of a telephone that her boss is out or has he told her to tell you that he is out?

Do you believe the engineer when he comes to repair your washing machine that the amount he is charging is the correct amount or is he trying to make a profit on the side?

OBEDIENCE

Do you believe your children when you suspect they have done something wrong?

Do you believe the shopkeeper when he tells you that he is sold out of something you want urgently?

Do you believe your Member of Parliament when he tells you he will do his best to improve your standard of living?

Do you believe your husband or wife when there are rumours going round that he or she has been unfaithful to you? Or do you believe the rumours?

All of the answers to these questions may well depend on how well you know the people you are talking to at that moment. Can their word be believed? Have you always found that what they have told you on previous occasions is the truth? If this is the case you are more likely to believe them on the next occasion they tell you anything.

It is the same when we read what Jesus says in the Bible. Do we believe what he says there? Everything he has said is borne out in the lives of Christians. Everything he said either was true at the time he said it or has come true since he said it or it will yet come to pass. And Jesus had quite a lot to say about Heaven and Hell.

Everything we read in the Bible has always been proved to be accurate. Some of the things people have queried over the years have now been proved to be correct.

God's word can be trusted.

When we acknowledge that, we are on our way to believing in Jesus as Saviour and Lord.

But where is Heaven?

After Jesus had been raised from the dead and had appeared to his disciples he told them to wait in Jerusalem until what we

71

now know as Pentecost or Whitsun. Some ten days before this event on the day we now call Ascension Day Jesus spoke to them for the last time while he was here on earth.

And when he had said this, as they were looking on, he was lifted up, and a cloud took him out of their sight. And while they were gazing into heaven as he went, behold, two men stood by them in white robes, and said, "Men of Galilee, why do you stand looking into heaven? This Jesus, who was taken up from you into heaven, will come in the same way as you saw him go into heaven." (Acts 1 v 9-11 RSV).

Does this mean that heaven is just above the clouds? Of course not!

We have to remember that the disciples were limited in their understanding of cosmic facts and even today we don't understand all that is in the universe.

Yes, the disciples were looking up but when Jesus reached the cloud he disappeared from their sight.

So is heaven up there, some way beyond the blue? And if so, which way? Do you take the first turning left at Pluto?

Again, of course not!

Do you remember the comment of one of the Russian astronauts when he was out in space, that he had proved that God did not exist because he could not see him?

His problem was not bad eyesight but incorrect theology!

Apart from anything else we already know that we cannot see God until we meet with Him in heaven.

To that selfsame question put by Philip,

"Lord, show us the Father, and we shall be satisfied." Jesus said to him, "Have I been with you so long, and yet you do not know me, Philip? He who has seen me has seen the Father; how can you say, 'Show us the Father?' Do you not believe that I am in the Father and the Father in me? The words that I say to you I do not speak on my own authority; but the Father who dwells in me does His works. Believe me that I am in the Father and the Father in me; or else believe me for the sake of the works themselves." (John 14 v 8-11 RSV).

So Jesus was God in the flesh while he was here on earth.

While he lived on earth in the region of Judea and Galilee he was subject to all the human limitations that we experience but without the sin because he was obedient to everything that God, his Father in Heaven, wanted him to do.

After his resurrection Jesus was no longer limited to his physical earthly body but possessed a heavenly spiritual body.

This enabled him to come and go as he pleased – hence his appearances to the disciples in the upper room and by the Sea of Galilee.

So where is Heaven?

It may well be a great deal nearer than we sometimes think.

It is a place where, as we have already seen, angels live.

At the present time, the fallen angels, those who have pledged their allegiance to the Devil, Satan, coexist alongside those who were faithful to God.

In the New Testament we read that Jesus confronted demons and had to cast them out of people. The disciples also had power to do this and even today there are ordinary Christians who have cast out demons from people who were possessed with them.

Now this is where I digress from the pages of Scripture but I believe that Heaven is a place, but it is not a place like England or Canada or even a planet that we haven't yet discovered but is in a different dimension and because of this we are unable to see it with our physical eyes. It could well be around us and certainly there have been people who have been aware of the presence of angels, and even Jesus, in the same room as themselves.

It is something exciting to which all those who have responded to the call to believe in Jesus as Lord and Saviour look forward to with great anticipation. Heaven is a place which will be better than anything we have ever experienced here on earth.

The entry to Heaven is through the gate called Death but it is not something to be feared by the Christian. For the non-Christian that is another story when we come to look under the heading called Hell.

Who, then, will be in Heaven?

Certainly there will be no evil there.

On the Mount of Transfiguration the disciples witnessed Jesus speaking with Moses and Elijah. They will be in Heaven.

Jesus himself spoke about Abraham, Isaac and Jacob and all the prophets in the Kingdom of Heaven. They will be there.

At the Passover meal Peter asked Jesus where he was going. Jesus replied that Peter couldn't follow him at that moment in time but later on.

Jesus then said, ' "Let not your hearts be troubled; believe in God, believe also in me. In my Father's house are many rooms; if it were not so, would I have told you that I go to prepare a place for you? And when I go and prepare a place for you, I will come again and will take you to myself, that where I am you may be also." ' (John 14 v 1-3 RSV).

This is one of the great passages to be found in the Bible. A tremendous help and encouragement to those who are on the threshold of death but also thrilling for all Christians to know that the future after death has been taken care of. With that hope beyond the grave how much more exciting, satisfying and comforting it is to live out the remainder of our lives here on earth. To those who have been bereaved and whose friends and relatives were Believers what a joy to know they are safe in the presence of God Himself. But more than that the certainty of knowing that one day they will meet again in Heaven.

Those who love Jesus as Lord and Saviour never say goodbye for the last time. For the Christian a funeral service is a service of joy and hope for the bereaved loved ones even though, inevitably, there is sorrow at parting for the moment but what a reunion there is going to be one day.

So in Heaven will be all those Old Testament people to whom righteousness was imputed and after Jesus came preaching the Gospel of repentance, all those who have committed their lives to him in faith and trust.

There is not a two-tier level of Christianity, those who are Christians and those who are Born Again Christians, because all Christians must be born again as Jesus told Nicodemus.

We may also think we know who are not in the Kingdom of Heaven but that is not for us to judge, that is God's prerogative.

What is certain is that God's judgement will be perfect. His decisions will be accurate and just and every individual will one day stand before Him to be judged. Jesus will be standing between God and the individual because man cannot look on God and live because of his sin. If the individual knows Jesus as his Saviour, Jesus will step aside and then he will be in the presence of God Himself because by accepting the atoning death of Jesus on the cross for himself he has become righteous, not by anything he has done but by believing in Jesus as his Lord and Saviour.

When Jesus was crucified on the cross at Calvary there were two criminals crucified alongside him, one on either side.

> One of the criminals who were hanged railed at him, saying, "Are you not the Christ? Save yourself and us!" But the other rebuked him, saying, "Do you not fear God, since you are under the same sentence of condemnation? And we indeed justly; for we are receiving the due rewards of our deeds; but this man has done nothing wrong." And he said, "Jesus, remember me when you come in your kingly power." And he said to him, "Truly, I say to you, today you will be with me in Paradise." (Luke 23 v 39-43 RSV).

This criminal will also be in Heaven. He could hardly have left it later. Not everyone who says, 'I'll make a decision to accept Jesus as my Saviour when I know I'm dying.' will do that because no one knows when that might be. Now is the time to make that decision. Tomorrow may be too late.

The second criminal made no such request and Jesus said no comforting words to him.

There are no comforting words for those who knowingly reject Jesus as their Saviour.

For the non-Believer, existence beyond the grave is a different matter.

His destination is Hell.

Hell

What is Hell?

Hell is a place where the Devil and his Fallen Angels are.

Hell is a place where God is not.

Hell is a place where Jesus is not.

Hell is a place where the Holy Spirit is not.

Hell is a place where the angels are not – unless they are the fallen ones.

Hell is a place where those who have rejected Jesus as their Lord and Saviour are.

Hell is a place of unmitigated evil.

Hell is a place of Eternal punishment. Whether there are degrees of punishment is an open question but one that does not concern the Believer.

Hell is a place of separation from God, not annihilation.

Hell is a place of Eternal pain. Whether that is physical or mental is another open question but again one that will not concern the Believer in Heaven but should motivate him to communicate the Gospel while he is still alive on earth so that those who are not Believers might not perish but have Eternal Life.

Hell is a place where parting is permanent.

Hell is a place of unrelieved remorse.

Hell is a place where those who are there can see what they should have done but are unable to do it because there is a great gulf fixed between them and God and there is no way across. The only access was through Jesus Christ and the pathway had to be trod whilst they were alive on earth. Jesus said to ' "enter by the narrow gate; for the gate is wide and the way is easy, that leads to destruction, and those who enter by it are many. For the gate is narrow and the way is hard, that leads to life, and those who find it are few."' (Matthew 7 v 13-14 RSV).

Hell is, of course, the very opposite of Heaven.

Hell is a place where, once there, no pathway will be found that will enable anyone to leave and enter Heaven. The gulf that is fixed is a permanent one.

Despite the belief of some there is no scriptural evidence at all of a place called Purgatory. There is no doctrine of Purgatory at all in the Bible. It is based on tradition and not scripture.

If we allow tradition to enter the discussion as a basis of faith and belief then there would be no end to the arguments involved.

Because there is no such place as Purgatory then praying for the dead in order to get them out of Hell is pointless because the dead are either in Heaven already or under God's judgement. In either case our prayers are not effective once a person has died.

Where is Hell?

Similarly to Heaven, and here the similarity ends, I believe it will be in a different dimension, a spiritual dimension.

As the Holy Spirit lives in the lives of those who have committed their lives to Jesus Christ so others can be possessed by evil spirits.

This is like the man who lived among the tombs in the country of the Gerasenes. He was possessed by a demon or unclean spirit. Jesus cast out the unclean spirit and it entered the pigs who were nearby who then rushed down a steep bank into the sea and were drowned. This spirit, or spirits, because they were called Legion, were then released to spend eventually an eternity in Hell.

OBEDIENCE

There are those who say that Hell will be a place of fellowship and friendship. I doubt it. Jesus said, '"Do not fear those who kill the body but cannot kill the soul; rather fear him who can destroy both soul and body in Hell."' (Matthew 10 v 28 RSV).

Hell will not be a place where comforts will be experienced and friendships made. Hell will be Hell!

Jesus gave many warnings against Hell. No one, on reading the Bible, can claim that they haven't been warned about the dangers of Hell. It will be their personal choice if they end up there.

Every winter in this country there are notices posted alongside ponds warning about the dangers of stepping on the ice. Tragically, every winter, children and adults are drowned because they ignore the warning signs. It was their choice that they went on to the ice, even if they weren't thinking logically.

Jesus said,

"If your hand, or your foot causes you to sin, cut it off and throw it from you; it is better for you to enter life maimed or lame than with two hands or two feet to be thrown into the eternal fire. And if your eye causes you to sin, pluck it out and throw it from you; it is better for you to enter life with one eye than with two eyes to be thrown into the hell of fire." (Matthew 18 v 8-9 RSV).

Jesus is not, of course, recommending that we gouge out our eyes or amputate our hands or feet but is warning against the dangers of being lured into sin whether it's by looking at something with our eyes or doing something with our hands or going somewhere with our feet. 'Keep away from doing wrong,' Jesus is saying to his hearers.

Hell will be a loss of hope. 'When the wicked dies, his hope perishes, and the expectation of the godless comes to nought.' (Proverbs 11 v 7 RSV).

When hope is gone, what has life got to hold?

Many prisoners captured during the Second World War stated that as long as they had the hope of seeing their wives and loved ones again they could stand the privations of imprisonment however harsh the regime. But when they heard that their wives had been unfaithful all hope had gone and there was no more reason for living. Hope had gone.

Every Saturday, millions of people watch the draw for the lottery, hoping that their numbers will come up, making them instant millionaires. Let's do away with the idea that they do it for fun. People do it to become rich in the hope that all their problems will be solved with six little balls coming up in the right order! Hope based on a false premise. Jesus talked about the danger of riches and how hard it is for a rich person to enter the Kingdom of Heaven. Not that they are unable to but that their wealth so often stands in their way. Riches become their god and they worship at the altar of their bank balance. Remember, banks have been known to collapse!

There are those who hope that God will save everyone in the end. 'How can a God of love allow anyone to suffer the pangs of Hell?' is often the quote you hear. If everyone will be saved in the end, then Hell becomes an irrelevance. That is, however, not what Jesus said and not the teaching of the Bible.

It is not enough to imagine in your mind what a place is like. You might have to go there to find out.

Some forty or more years ago I had a picture in my mind of a beautiful place in the heart of North Wales. It had a name that sounded picturesque. It was called Blaenau Ffestiniog. The first time I went there was in a coach on a grey, dank, drizzly day. If you've ever been there you may understand that my dreams of a pretty village in idyllic surroundings were somewhat shattered, to say the least! To save upsetting all the present residents I have to say that I have been there subsequently and found it to be not so depressing as on that first visit, even though the sun wasn't shining!

It isn't enough to think in our own minds what will happen at death. We need to refer to God's word, the Bible, to find out. It's no good hoping that everyone will go to Heaven in the end and no one will go to Hell because the Bible states categorically that that is not the case. We can ignore it but when we get there it will be too late to put ourselves into reverse gear. The road to Hell is a one-way street and when we arrive there, there will be no turning round and going back. We have to take the right road while we live here on earth.

So the hope that God will save everybody in the end is merely a hope, as we have seen, not based on the Bible.

Yes, God is a God of Love but He is also a Holy God and a God of Justice.

Because God is Holy He is unable to tolerate sin as we have already discovered. God's Holiness means that anything that is evil can never be found in Heaven. God has, however, provided the way to overcome sin and evil by the sacrifice of Jesus on the cross at Calvary. All who believe in Jesus as Lord and Saviour are saved from that journey into Hell.

So God is love and God is Holy but God is also a Judge and we can rest assured that His judgement will be perfect.

No one will find themselves in the wrong place. It is certain that anyone who finds themselves in Hell will deserve to be there. God will not prevent anyone from going there if they choose that path.

God gave us free will. That's what happened in the garden of Eden when Adam and Eve exercised that free will to disobey God and eat of the tree of knowledge of good and evil. Man has rebelled against God's authority and disobeyed Him. Man has become a sinner and God's righteous anger is always against sin. It is unrepentant sinners that are sent to Hell. Jesus makes it clear that unrepentant sinners are in more danger than even those who were engaged in sexual misdemeanours in Sodom. '"And you, Capernaum, will you be exalted to Heaven? You shall be brought down to Hades. For if the mighty works done in you had been done in Sodom, it would have remained until this day. But I tell you that it shall be more tolerable on the day of judgment for the land of Sodom than for you."' (Matthew 11 v 23-24 RSV).

In his letter to the Church at Galatia Paul makes a list of how human beings behave without God. 'Now the works of the flesh are plain: immorality, impurity, licentiousness, idolatry, sorcery, enmity, strife, jealousy, anger, selfishness, dissension, party spirit, envy, drunkenness, carousing and the like. I warn you, as I warned you before, that those who do such things shall not inherit the Kingdom of God.' (Galatians 5 v 19-21 RSV).

So we're all on our way to Hell unless we believe in the Gospel, that is, the Good News that God sent His Son, Jesus Christ, into the world to save sinners, which is all of us, because we've all sinned and come short of the standard God requires. We need to be forgiven and we'll look at this in another chapter.

Angels and Demons

In pre-creation God existed with a number of spiritual beings we call angels.

It was a spiritual existence, a perfect existence about which we obviously know very little.

We do know, however, that Satan or Lucifer was cast out of this Paradise. 'How you are fallen from Heaven, O Day Star, son of Dawn! How you are cut down to the ground, you who laid the nations low!' (Isaiah 14 v 12 RSV). Other versions mention Lucifer by name.

Other angels also rebelled against God and were cast out. These were the demons Jesus confronted from time to time and who obviously recognized Jesus. They would have known him personally in Heaven!

We can only guess at why they rebelled. Ultimately it would come back to not accepting the authority of God and wanting to do as they pleased for themselves.

Satan and his fellow evil spirits have no opportunity to repent and confess their sin, an opportunity given to the vilest of human beings whilst they exist here on earth. They have no opportunity to be forgiven.

So God created another Paradise in which He placed Adam and Eve. For how long they lived there before they gave in to the temptation to eat from the tree of knowledge of good and evil we do not know. Their disobedience separated them from God because to eat from this tree had been forbidden.

Each time it is disobedience that separates from God. That disobedience is called sin. Sin always separates. God and sin are unable to coexist because God is Holy.

Satan existed with the Christian proof that so many people ask for before they will believe in Jesus as Saviour. He knew Jesus in Eternity. But he still rebelled against God and cut himself off from fellowship with God forever. There is no way back for Satan.

We should be eternally thankful that that is not the case for us humans.

Following Adam and Eve's sin in the Garden of Eden, God was providing a way of forgiveness for us human beings.

Forgiveness

There's a way back to God from the dark paths of sin;
There's a way that is open and you may go in.
At Calvary's cross is where you begin,
When you come as a sinner to Jesus.

So runs the chorus that some of us may have learned as a child. The words may be simple but they contain a profound truth.

Without forgiveness there can be no way back to God.

Without repentance there can be no forgiveness.

Without obedience there can be no repentance.

As we have already seen, sin separates.

We are cut off from fellowship with God by man's sin and there is no way back from man's side. Only God is able to provide a way back to fellowship with Himself.

In the Old Testament the only way to do this was by sacrifices. It was called Atonement.

The sacrifices were animals, quite often a goat.

When Abraham was about to sacrifice his son Isaac, God

provided a ram instead and Abraham offered it up as a burnt offering in place of his son.

When Moses was going to lead the Israelites out from captivity in Egypt it was a lamb without blemish that was sacrificed and its blood was put on the doorposts and lintels of the houses in which they were eating the lamb so that the angel of death would pass over. It became known as the Lord's Passover.

Jesus, on the night before he died on the cross, took this Passover meal and gave it a new meaning. It became known as the Lord's Supper and Jesus told his disciples to celebrate this meal in remembrance of him. 'Now as they were eating, Jesus took bread, and blessed, and broke it, and gave it to the disciples and said, "Take, eat; this is my body." And he took a cup, and when he had given thanks he gave it to them, saying, "Drink of it, all of you; for this is my blood of the covenant, which is poured out for many for the forgiveness of sins."' (Matthew 26 v 26-28 RSV).

Christians, everywhere, celebrate the Lord's Supper, remembering all that Jesus has done for them when he gave his life on the cross; how he became the sacrifice for our sin. It was on the cross that Jesus uttered the words, '"Father forgive them, for they don't know what they're doing."'

When Jesus started his ministry, he came into Galilee and preached the message that God wanted him to give. He said, '"The time is fulfilled, and the Kingdom of God is at hand; repent, and believe in the Gospel."'

That was the difference between Judas Iscariot and Simon Peter.

Judas had betrayed Jesus to the authorities and never

repented about what he had done and he went out and committed suicide.

Peter wept when he realised he had denied, three times, that he even knew Jesus and he repented of what he had done. After the Resurrection Jesus forgave Peter and restored him back into fellowship.

In order, therefore, to be restored back into fellowship, we have to obey what God says and believe the Gospel, that is, the Good News that Jesus died on the cross for our sin and if we do that we are brought back into fellowship with Him.

In the prayer that Jesus taught his disciples part of it states that as we ask for forgiveness from God so in a similar manner we are to forgive others.

Peter asked Jesus on one occasion how many times should a person be forgiven. ' "Lord, how often shall my brother sin against me, and I forgive him? As many as seven times?" Jesus said to him, "I do not say to you seven times but seventy times seven." '

Jesus did not mean that a person was to forgive another 490 times and then he needn't forgive him any more. He meant forgiveness was to be limitless.

Jesus went on to explain that the Kingdom of Heaven could be compared with a King who wished to settle accounts with his servants.

When he began the reckoning, one was brought to him who owed him ten thousand talents; and as he could not pay, his lord ordered him to be sold, with his wife and children and all that he had, and payment to be made. So the servant fell on his knees, imploring him, "Lord, have patience with me, and I will pay you everything." And out of pity for him the lord of that servant released him and forgave him the debt. But that same servant as he went out, came upon one of his fellow servants who owed him a hundred denarii; and seizing him by the throat he said, "Pay what you owe." So his fellow servant fell down and besought him, "Have patience with me, and I will pay you." He refused and went and put him in prison till he should pay the debt. When his fellow servants saw what had taken place, they were greatly distressed, and they went and reported to their lord all that had taken place. Then his lord summoned him and said to him, "You wicked servant! I forgave you all that debt because you besought me; and should not you have had mercy on your fellow servant, as I had mercy on you?" And in anger his lord delivered him to the jailers, till he should pay all his debt. So also my Heavenly Father will do to every one of you, if you do not forgive your brother from your heart. (Matthew 18 v 24-35 RSV).

As God forgives us so we must forgive others who do us wrong. If we harbour resentment we destroy ourselves. We have already mentioned Enniskillen when the I.R.A. let off a bomb killing several people. One of those killed was the daughter of a man by the name of Gordon Wilson who said that he forgave those who had killed his daughter in so dreadful a manner. What was going on in his mind at that moment we may never know but what he did was a Christian thing to do and followed the teaching of Jesus in his Sermon on the Mount. It did not mean that those who perpetrated the crime should not have been brought to justice, if caught and punished for their crime.

When Jesus spoke about not resisting one who is evil and not striking anyone back he is talking about personal vengeance when an act has been committed against an individual. He was not discussing the Roman Government's responsibility to maintain Law and Order. If he had been, the Pharisees would have had him up before the Roman authorities as quickly as possible in order to get rid of him before his ministry had barely started.

These passages do not mean that we should not defend our family, our property or our country but that we should not attempt to get our own back personally.

Justice

We have already seen that God is a Judge. He is also a just Judge. Everything He does is exactly right.

Our judicial system is at the moment very much in the news. The general public, and rightly so, are concerned about the level of crime and violent crime in particular. Two of the things we are hearing about are Zero Tolerance and Three Strikes and Out. Should we copy the United States and incorporate these two methods into our way of clearing up crime? From all accounts, it appears that it is working and crime is beginning to decrease because of these two methods being used. Are they just? Are they right? Should we use them here in the United Kingdom?

We should try to find a just punishment for any crime committed.

Now, an infringement of the law may take only a few minutes or even a few seconds. It has been estimated that the average burglary takes only a few minutes to carry out. Are we suggesting that the punishment should also take a few minutes? That would be ridiculous. You might as well not bother at all.

We return to the Old Testament's 'an eye for an eye and a

tooth for a tooth' if we want to be just. The difficulty is in actually carrying out the just sentence. The public either deem the criminal to have been dealt with too leniently or too severely, depending on whose side you are arguing from.

In the days just after the Second World War I used to go and watch professional football matches every Saturday afternoon, (and Saturday afternoon is the time to be playing football, but that's another matter!) unless I was playing myself. Living within almost walking distance of Q.P.R., Brentford, Fulham and Chelsea I was spoilt for choice, and the other London clubs were within easy travelling distance on the Underground.

My father took me to watch Q.P.R. when I was about nine years old, hence that is the team I still support although I no longer attend matches for a number of reasons. I would go in all weathers, rain or snow, and I've watched a number of games in the snow, sometimes queuing up for hours to get into the ground to stand. In those days there were large crowds, most of them standing. Supporters were not segregated, bad language was almost unheard of, obscene chants were unknown, there was no danger of violence erupting either on or off the pitch and the football was much more exciting, at least that's my opinion! In those days when I was watching there was no such thing as Red and Yellow cards. If a player offended then the referee took his name and noted it and either booked him or sent him off.

Now I know memory can play you tricks, but I have no recollection of any players being sent off or even their names taken although I suppose it must have happened on the odd occasion. Today, and I avidly watch Match of the Day on television on Saturday evenings whenever I am at home, not a match goes by, or so it seems, without a player or players being shown the Yellow or Red cards. And what happens? – a protestation of innocence from most of them. They can't understand what the referee has seen. 'It wasn't me Ref. I'm innocent – you've gone over the top!' And when we get the analysis from the experts as they sum up the game, with the help of slow-motion cameras, they also make their judgement as to whether the punishment was justified or not. 'We were robbed!' is the comment often heard from the players or managers after a game is finished.

What I am sure about is that in all the matches in which I played, covering a period of about twenty years, no player on either side was ever booked or sent off and yet we enjoyed the matches and played just as hard as today.

Football is a microcosm of the world outside, then and now. In fact, in today's climate, it has got so bad at times that some players are taking other players to court for violent conduct, and it's meant to be a sport!

And it's not much better in cricket – the sport of gentlemen!

We now have a third umpire to see that justice is done for run-outs, and to be fair, it appears to work and there are no miscarriages of justice.

We can be sure that there will be no miscarriages of justice from God. His judgement is, and will be, perfect.

When the time comes for us to face the judgement seat of God everything will be laid bare. We won't be able to say, 'It wasn't me God.' Or if we do then He will be able to prove to us that it was.

Judgement

God's judgement will bring God's justice.

We would always like the punishment to fit the crime but the problem comes when we don't believe it does. So then we want to take the situation into our own hands and administer our own punishment, but that would be wrong.

In our country impartial judges and juries hear a case and the jury finds the defendant guilty or not guilty and the judge passes the sentence.

At the Day of Judgement the sentence will be passed, not by an impartial judge, however skilled and knowledgeable he may be, but by an all-knowing and all-loving God who will take into account every little detail which will be recorded and played back.

Thirty years ago we might have queried how God could keep account of every detail of our life. Video and tape recorders have helped us understand a little more, perhaps, how this can be done. God's video and tape recorders have been running from the beginning of time and the tapes will not default or come to the end until we die or Jesus comes again.

'That's going to take a long time,' you might say. True, but there's all eternity for the judgement to take place so that won't be a problem!

God's judgement will be God's perfect justice.

Paul takes up the subject of not trying to get your own back when he says, 'Beloved, never avenge yourselves, but leave it to the wrath of God; for it is written, "Vengeance is mine, I will repay, says the Lord."' (Romans 12 v 19 RSV). Where is that written? In the Old Testament in both Leviticus and Deuteronomy.

Does that mean that God is just waiting for the time to get His own back on everyone who has done wrong? Is He an avenging God? No, of course not, but what it does mean is that every wrong God knows about and He will punish the offenders in His own time.

Do you have a good memory?

Or do you find it difficult to remember appointments, times and dates?

If you are in the latter category you will not be alone. Many people forget things.

When I worked in a bank, you had to remember every transaction that was carried out and the only way to be sure that nothing was missed was to record it in a book somewhere. Nothing was committed to memory but nothing was ever forgotten because every item was recorded.

When I was in the teaching profession one of the phrases that I coined was 'write it down.'

Those of you reading this book who are, or were, teachers will know the number of times that children forget to bring in their homework or forget their P.E. kit or fail to tell their parents something even when they have been given a note to take home.

Our memories are fallible but one of the ways to help them is to record what we have to do or remember somewhere as long as we remember where we have put the note!

An even better way is to purchase a diary and record all the events we have to remember. Maybe more birthdays and anniversaries would not be forgotten if this happened! However, don't lose your diary or you could be in worse trouble!

How will God remember?

Apart from video and tape recorders, already mentioned, a written record is kept called the Lamb's Book of Life, and this will never be lost.

The Book of Revelation gives an account of the Last Judgement where we can also read about this Book of Life.

> And I saw the dead, great and small, standing before the throne, and books were opened. Also another book was opened, which is the Book of Life. And the dead were judged by what was written in the books, by what they had done. And the sea gave up the dead in it, Death and Hades gave up the dead in them, and all were judged by what they had done. Then Death and Hades were thrown into the lake of fire. This is the second death, the lake of fire; and if any one's name was not found written in the Book of Life, he was thrown into the lake of fire. (Revelation 20 v 12-15 RSV).

All of us will have to stand before the judgement seat of Christ. There will be no escape from the van taking us to court. We will be there.

If you've ever been involved in any way in a trial at the Old Bailey you will have experienced the solemnity of the occasion. Very little laughter in Court.

There will be no laughter at all in the Court of Justice when we stand before the judgement of God because this judgement will be final and eternal.

We shall all be brought face to face with God the Father and God the Son from whom there will be no escape. We can't escape over the fence because there is no fence. We can't put up a ladder to climb over the wall and escape in a van on the other side provided for the occasion like escaping from Wormwood

Scrubs because there will be no ladder, there will be no wall and there will be no van.

Notice that there is more than one Book.

First of all let's deal with the Book of Life. In this Book are written all the names of those who have trusted in Jesus Christ as Lord and Saviour. In other words those who have been obedient to the way provided by God for salvation. Those names found in the other books are not saved from the penalty of sin and death.

Paul and Silas were in prison in Philippi because they had been preaching about Jesus and had freed a slave girl from a spirit of divination and the slave girl's owners had lost their living because she was now in her right mind, so they persuaded the magistrates that Paul and Silas were trouble-makers. Then there was an earthquake, the foundations of the prison were shaken and the doors were opened and everyone's chains were loosed. The jailer thought they had escaped and was about to kill himself because he knew he would be in trouble when Paul shouted that they were still there and told him not to harm himself. He was trembling with fear and fell down before Paul and Silas and said to them, '"Men, what must I do to be saved?" And they said, "Believe in the Lord Jesus, and you will be saved, you and your household."' (Acts 16 v 30-31 RSV). The jailer and his family became Believers and were baptized that very night. He rejoiced with all his family that he had believed in God.

The names of that jailer and his family will be found in the Book of Life because they believed in Jesus Christ as their Lord and Saviour.

That is the only criterion for the name of anyone to be found there.

There will be no spelling mistakes. There will be no omissions. No one who should be there will be left out. No one who shouldn't be there will be in it by mistake. God's records, as are His judgements, are perfect.

The other books contain the records of the works of those whose names are not written in the Book of Life.

We might ask why there is any need to look at the works of those who are lost. They are recorded in order to show the gravity of their sins in order to determine what punishment is applicable. Even the sea gives up its dead and the graves also, as well as those who were cremated. God's video tape will be played back and no one will escape from judgement.

All whose names are in these books, that is, those whose names are not found in the Book of Life, will be cast into the lake of fire. This means that they will be separated from God eternally in a conscious and never-ending torment. Whether this torment is in reality burning in fire or a torment of the soul or 'merely' an unending boredom is a nice theological debating point, but whichever it is or a combination of all three it will be Hell.

Second Coming of Jesus

Jesus came once into this world when he was born as a baby at Bethlehem. His birth was foretold in the Old Testament.

Jesus himself said that he would be coming again. ' "When I go and prepare a place for you, I will come again and will take you to myself, that where I am you may be also." ' (John 14 v 3 RSV). He also said, ' "But of that day or that hour no one knows, not even the angels in heaven, nor the Son, but only the father. Take heed, watch; for you do not know when the time will come."' (Mark 13 v 32-33).

He did give indications of what we were to look out for including wars, famines and earthquakes. He said that many false prophets will arise and there will be people claiming to be Christ who will lead others astray.

All of these have already happened on many occasions.

He also said, ' "And this gospel of the Kingdom will be preached throughout the whole world, as a testimony to all nations; and then the end will come."' (Matthew 24 v 14 RSV).

Certainly the Gospel has been preached in every continent and I doubt if there are many countries which it hasn't reached, so in those terms the Gospel has already been preached to every nation, but one of the criteria for the Gospel to be understood by everybody is to have the Bible translated into the language of the people. This is being done by Wycliffe Bible Translators and the Bible Society. There are said to be about five thousand or more languages in the world but many of these are spoken by a very few, sometimes just hundreds.

So if the Gospel hasn't yet been preached throughout the whole world we can't be very far off.

When all these things have been done, the end of the world as we know it will come.

What we can never do is to hazard a guess at the date. Too many cranks have tried that and then always have to make an excuse when the day goes by and nothing has happened.

That doesn't mean to say that we can totally ignore the warning of Jesus because it will come when we are least expecting it.

OBEDIENCE

Paul wrote to the Church at Thessalonica and told them, 'But as to the times and the seasons, brethren, you have no need to have anything written to you. For you yourselves know well that the day of the Lord will come like a thief in the night.' (1 Thessalonians 5 v 1-2 RSV).

In other words we need to be prepared for Jesus' second coming but we will never know when it will be.

When Moses was going to lead the Israelites out of captivity in Egypt he told them to be ready and to eat their meal quickly. It was more important to do that than to think about their digestion on this occasion! ' "In this manner you shall eat it; your loins girded, your sandals on your feet, and your staff in your hand; and you shall eat it in haste." ' (Exodus 12 v 11 RSV).

When the time came to move there was going to be no time to do anything else.

If we are catching an early morning flight to go on holiday I guess most of us are ready the night before with our cases packed, waiting for the person who is going to take us to the airport. When that ring on the doorbell comes, we pick up our luggage and get in the car. There is no time for any delay, we don't want to miss the plane. There may not be another one for a week and it would cause our holiday to descend into chaos.

Paul wrote the following to the Church at Corinth; 'Lo! I tell you a mystery. We shall not all sleep, but we shall all be changed, in a moment, in the twinkling of an eye, at the last trumpet. For the trumpet will sound, and the dead will be raised imperishable, and we shall be changed.' (1 Corinthians 15 v 51-52 RSV).

How much more important it is to be ready for Jesus' second

coming. This will be even quicker and we won't need our passports!

It may be true, of course, that we are not alive when Jesus comes again but our death has the same effect as if he had come again. Time has gone and we are in eternity. It is too late to make any further decisions regarding our final destiny. It will be either Heaven or Hell and the choice will have been made by us. God never forces anyone into Heaven or Hell. He provides the way but we choose which way we go.

The Way Forward

I started this book with the thought of safety in mind. Safety on the roads, safety in the home, safety on the way to school, safety in the market place, safety at night, safety during the hours of daylight, safety out walking in the woods and safety in the crowded streets. I am ending it with the thought of our eternal safety; safety from the power of the Devil, Satan; safety from Eternal judgement; safety from the pangs of Hell.

Let's have a look at the way forward we can take to eradicate all the dangers that face us in all these different directions.

At the heart of safety is the word 'obedience'. The vast majority of problems are caused because people do not accept the rules of life and the rules of death.

At a simple level if cars were restricted to five miles per hour there would be very few fatal accidents. Obvious! But life in the end of the twentieth century has moved on a lot faster and it would be totally impractical to limit speed to that level. What then should the speed limit be? Personally, I believe that some of the speed limits are too fast and some are too slow. I believe that the criterion should be dangerous driving and any infringement thereof punished severely.

However, whatever I think is not really important. What is important is that we obey the rules of the road with consideration for other road users and pedestrians. Long before drink-driving became an offence in law, to drive after having consumed alcohol showed a disregard for other people on the road. The command in the Bible is to love our neighbour as ourselves and most people don't want to destroy themselves. 'Who is my neighbour?' was a question put to Jesus by a lawyer when he was trying to trick Jesus into saying something which would land him in trouble with the authorities.

It led to Jesus telling the story about the Samaritan who helped the man who fell among thieves on the road from Jerusalem to Jericho, a story that most people have heard about today, even if they don't attend Church!

In other words our neighbour is not just the person who lives next door but anyone with whom we come into contact.

I doubt if those who commit robbery or burglary give a moment's thought to the people whom they are robbing. If they do, then it is likely to be the idea that because they live in a house, however large or small, and have possessions the robber may not have, then they are only really sharing their goods with others who have a greater need. Thinking, but obverse thinking!

It would surprise me if many criminals of the armed robbery, mugging and burglary type come from a stable, two-parent family.

I should be even more surprised if many come from a Bible-Believing Christian family.

We need to come back to families whose precepts and beliefs and practices are firmly based on the Bible.

Bringing up children is a full-time, two-parent, male and female occupation.

Children need two parents, a mother and a father.

Every encouragement and incentive, including tax incentives should be given to families who are struggling to make ends meet, but no incentives, tax or otherwise should be given to individuals who set out deliberately to become a one-parent family.

It is a struggle even where there are two parents, but for a single mother it becomes almost impossible even though there are exceptions to every rule. The scenario normally goes something like the following: 'Get out of my sight; go and find something to do without bothering me.' The result is, when they get older, and older these days can start at a very early age, they are out on the streets, probably the mother doesn't know where they are and they begin to get into trouble. Finally, they end up doing something against the law and the process of a life of crime has begun. Now I admit this can also happen in two-parent families where both parents couldn't care less or can't be troubled how their offspring behave. Being parents is a full-time, twenty-four hours a day, seven days a week, fifty-two weeks a year occupation until they become adults. (Is eighteen too young? It was twenty-one in my day!) Even when they leave home they surely remain our responsibility until they are handed on to someone else in marriage and the process begins again. Such is the Biblical concept of marriage and how God intended it to be. That on so many occasions it didn't work out that way is not God's fault but man's sin and the Bible doesn't gloss over the facts but records them, but doesn't commend them. Disobedience once again.

The Bible tells us to care for the widow and the fatherless but says little about single mothers. It doesn't occur very often in the Bible because it was seen as being wrong to set out deliberately to have a child without being in a family situation.

Recently we have had a Member of Parliament accused of calling the children of an unmarried Parliamentary candidate of another party, bastards. Maybe he said it in an insensitive manner but sadly, that's what they are. How much better for couples to get married before having children and then the situation could not arise. Who is it who is in reality being insensitive to the children they beget?

Tax incentives and allowances for married couples should be far higher than for couples who are living together and not married. We make it sound so romantic today by referring to 'my partner' rather than 'my fornicator' or even 'my concubine'. At least that would be Biblical!

Monogamy is implicit in the lifestyle of Adam and Eve but it wasn't much further along the way when polygamy was adopted and appears not to be forbidden, at least in the Old Testament. Polygamy can often bring trouble as in the case of Abraham's wife, Sarah, and his handmaid, Hagar.

By the time Christ came there appears to be no continued authority or practice in the New Testament for polygamy or the owning of concubines in the Christian era.

In fact, in his Sermon on the Mount, Jesus comes down strongly for the sanctity of marriage. 'It was also said, "Whoever divorces his wife, let him give her a certificate of divorce." But I say to you that every one who divorces his wife, except on the ground of unchastity, makes her an adulteress; and whoever marries a divorced woman commits adultery!' (Matthew 5 v 31-32 RSV). Strong words.

In the present modern mixed-up tangled web of marriage, divorce and remarriage, the Christian Church has to accept the situation as it is found. Not God's original plan for lifelong marriage but the state as caused by man's sin and disobedience. Under today's law, someone who has been divorced, for whatever reason, and who has remarried, cannot return to the original wife, and the present marriage cannot be branded as an adulterous arrangement.

Paul talks about this situation in his letter to the Church at Corinth where there were many sexual problems to sort out.

> Do you not know that the unrighteous will not inherit the Kingdom of God? Do not be deceived; neither the immoral, nor idolaters, not adulterers, nor homosexuals, nor thieves, nor the greedy, nor drunkards, nor revilers, nor robbers will inherit the Kingdom of God. And such were some of you. But you were washed, you were sanctified, you were justified in the name of the Lord Jesus Christ and in the Spirit of our God. (1 Corinthians 6 v 9-11 RSV).

In other words, they were heading for life beyond the grave in Hell but because they have become Believers and have confessed their sin they are deemed to be righteous in the sight of God, not because of what they were, or even what they have done, but because they have accepted the atoning death of Jesus on the cross and have believed in him for their salvation.

Paul goes on to talk about the need to remain married to one wife or one husband.

In Biblical times the extended family would sometimes take care of those who were bereaved but there were still widows who needed assistance. This was the case as the number of disciples increased.

> Now in these days when the disciples were increasing in number, the Hellenists murmured against the Hebrews because their widows were neglected in the daily distribution. And the twelve summoned the body of the disciples and said, "It is not right that we should give up preaching the word of God to serve tables. Therefore, brethren, pick out from among you seven men of good repute, full of the Spirit and of wisdom, whom we may appoint to this duty. But we will devote ourselves to prayer and to the ministry of the word." (Acts 6 v 1-4 RSV).

What they said pleased everyone and both preaching the Gospel and helping those in need were done alongside each other but by different members of the Believers. So it should be today.

Obviously, where there is bereavement in a family, help will be needed, particularly where there are children to care for, but the deliberate creating of a one-parent situation should not be tolerated or encouraged.

As we have already seen, separation and divorce cause parenting problems which are not normally helped by remarriage. Families need to stay together in order that discipline can be maintained.

If this were the case I believe many of the problems of criminal activities we face today would be eradicated, although not all.

How do we reduce these that are included in the 'not all'?

By making the punishment fit the crime.

Obviously, if capital punishment is carried out, the criminal cannot offend again.

If prison is the prescribed punishment then the regime must be such that the offender, on release, never wants to go to prison for a second time. Prison must be humane and hygienic but never a place which is more comfortable than living in the community. There must also be a programme of rehabilitation.

For those who are a danger to the community then release must be considered very carefully, if at all.

To live in a democracy, free from danger, free from fear, then the criminal element must be taken out of society or be so reformed that there is no possibility of reoffending.

Then, perhaps, we can walk the streets, the subways, the parks, the woods with no fear of being attacked, robbed or raped.

We can live in our houses without having to erect high fences or fix elaborate security devices and maybe even leave our doors unlocked.

But that day will never come unless we elect Members of Parliament, of whatever political persuasion, who see Crime and Punishment as the key election issue in our country today.

It will never come unless Parliament sees Capital Punishment as one of the options available for maintaining Law and Order.

It will never come unless Judges and Magistrates pass sentences that fit the crime.

It will never come unless we return to God's original plan for marriage, where love, faithfulness and responsibility for the rearing of children are involved.

The End and the Beginning

Even then, we have to face the reality of death because of man's sin at the beginning of creation.

We will not live forever, as God intended.

The end of our life here on Earth is the beginning of our life in Eternity.

While the remedy for peace on earth, or peace in our nation, is the responsibility for the country as a whole as represented by Parliament, the remedy for peace in the life of an individual is that individual's direct response to the remedy provided by God through His Son, Jesus Christ.

That peace, and the certainty of Eternal Life in Heaven, will never come unless we believe in Jesus Christ as the Saviour of the world. As our Saviour. As my Saviour.

Yes, let's get 'Back to Basics'.